Math Contests For High School
Volume 1

School Years: 1977-78 through 1981-82

Steven R. Conrad ● **Daniel Flegler**

Published by MATH LEAGUE PRESS
Printed in the United States of America

Cover art by Nancy Tuttle Design

First Retitled & Reorganized Printing, 1992

Math League Press
P.O. Box 720
Tenafly, NJ 07670

ISBN 0-940805-08-1

Preface

Math Contests—High School, Volume 1 is the first volume in our series of problem books for high school students. This volume contains the 30 contests that were given during the 1977-78 through 1981-82 school years. The second volume contains the 54 contests given from 1982-83 through 1990-91. (You may use the form on page 70 to order any of our 6 contest books.)

These book gives classes, clubs, teams, and individuals diversified collections of high school math problems. All of these contests were used in regional interscholastic competition throughout the United States and Canada. Each contest was taken by about 80 000 students. In the contest section, each page contains a complete contest that can be worked during a 30-minute period. The convenient format makes this book easy to use in a class, a math club, or for just plain fun. In addition, detailed solutions for each contest also appear on a single page.

Every contest has questions from different areas of mathematics. The goal is to encourage interest in mathematics through solving *worthwhile* problems. Many students first develop an interest in mathematics through problem-solving activities such as these contests. On each contest, the last two questions are generally more difficult than the first four. The final question on each contest is intended to challenge the very best mathematics students. The problems require no knowledge beyond secondary school mathematics. No knowledge of calculus is required to solve any of these problems. From two to four questions on each contest are accessible to students with only a knowledge of elementary algebra.

This book is divided into four sections for ease of use by both students and teachers. The first section of the book contains the contests. Each contest contains six questions that can be worked in a 30-minute period. The second section of the book contains detailed solutions to all the contests. Often, several solutions are given for a problem. Where appropriate, notes about interesting aspects of a problem are mentioned on the solutions page. The third section of the book consists of a listing of the answers to each contest question. The last section of the book contains the difficulty rating percentages for each question. These percentages (based on actual student performance on these contests) determine the relative difficulty of each question.

You may prefer to consult the answer section rather than the solution section when first reviewing a contest. The authors believe that reworking a problem when the answer (but *not* the solution) is known often helps to better understand problem-solving techniques.

Revisions have been made to the wording of some problems for the sake of clarity and correctness. The authors welcome comments you may have about either the questions or the solutions. Though we believe there are no errors in this book, each of us agrees to blame the other should any errors be found!

Steven R. Conrad & Daniel Flegler, contest authors

Acknowledgments

For her continued patience and understanding, special thanks to Marina Conrad, whose only mathematical skill, an important one, is the ability to count the ways.

For her lifetime support and encouragement, special thanks to Mildred Flegler.

To Paul Campbell, Beloit College, Beloit, Wisconsin; Richard Gibbs, Fort Lewis College, Durango, Colorado; and Michael Selby, University of Windsor, Windsor, Ontario; we offer our gratitude for advice and assistance over the years.

To Alan Feldman, who suggested several stylistic changes from our previous edition to this one, we offer our thanks.

To Martin Rudolph, for his pervasive influence.

To Brian and Keith Conrad, who again did an awesome proofreading job, thanks!

Table Of Contents

The Contests
October, 1977 – April, 1982

Contest Number 1   November 15, 1977

Name _____ Grade Level _____ Score _____

Time Limit: 30 minutes   *Answer Column*

1-1.   The I.Q. of a Martian varies directly with the square of the number of tentacles it has. If a Martian with 5 tentacles has an I.Q. of 75, what is the I.Q. of a Martian with 8 tentacles?

1-1.

1-2.   A plane is partitioned into 2 regions by 1 line and into 4 regions by 2 intersecting lines. Into how many disjoint regions do 5 coplanar lines partition the plane, if no 2 of the lines are parallel and no 3 of them are concurrent?

1-2.

1-3.   Two noncongruent circles are externally tangent. Each base of an isosceles trapezoid is a diameter of one of the circles. If the distance between the centers of the circles is 8, what is the area of the trapezoid?

1-3.

1-4.   When written in base fifty-one or base one hundred eighty-seven, the expansion of $\frac{1}{n}$ terminates. If n is an integer greater than 1, what is the least possible value of n? (Write your answer in base ten.)

1-4.

1-5.   What are all ordered pairs of integers (x,y) which satisfy
$$x^3 + y^3 - 3x^2 + 6y^2 + 3x + 12y + 6 = 0?$$

1-5.

1-6.   In $\triangle ABC$, $AC = 18$, and D is the point on $\overline{AC}$ for which $AD = 5$. Perpendiculars drawn from D to $\overline{AB}$ and $\overline{CB}$ have lengths of 4 and 5 respectively. What is the area of $\triangle ABC$?

1-6.

Contest Number 2   **December 13, 1977**

Name _____ Grade Level _____ Score _____

Time Limit: 30 minutes	Answer Column
2-1. The 4th term of a sequence is 4 and the 6th term is 6. Every term after the 2nd is the sum of the 2 preceding terms. What is the 8th term of this sequence?	2-1.
2-2. The circle circumscribed about regular heptagon $ABCDEFG$ has an area of 196π. If the bisectors of angles A and D intersect at P, what is the length of $\overline{AP}$?	2-2.
2-3. One urn contains 1 liter of water, while a second urn is empty. After $\frac{1}{2}$ of the water in the first is emptied into the second, $\frac{1}{3}$ of the water in the second is returned to the first. Then, $\frac{1}{4}$ of the contents of the first is poured into the second, followed by a return of $\frac{1}{5}$ of the contents of the second into the first. At each successive pouring, from alternate urns, the denominator of the fractional part poured increases by 1. How many liters of water remain in the first urn right after the 1977th pouring?	2-3.
2-4. The elements of set B are all the possible subsets of set A. Set B has 16 subsets. What is the number of elements in set A?	2-4.
2-5. For how many ordered triples of unequal positive integers (x,y,z) is a positive integral value attained by $$\frac{x}{(x-y)(x-z)} + \frac{y}{(y-x)(y-z)} + \frac{z}{(z-x)(z-y)}?$$	2-5.
2-6. In parallelogram $ABCD$, the bisector of $\angle ABC$ intersects $\overline{AD}$ at P. If $PD = 5$, $BP = 6$, and $CP = 6$, what is the value of AB?	2-6.

HIGH SCHOOL MATHEMATICS CONTESTS

P.O. Box 720, Tenafly, New Jersey 07670

Contest Number 3   **January 10, 1978**

Name _____ Grade Level _____ Score _____

Time Limit: 30 minutes   *Answer Column*

3-1. One diagonal of a square serves as the shorter base of a trapezoid, and a line through one of the vertices of the square contains the other base. The legs of the trapezoid are extensions of two sides of the square. If the area of the square is 2800, what is the area of the trapezoid?

3-1.

3-2. What is the real value of x which satisfies

$$5x + 3\sqrt{x} - 2 = 0?$$

3-2.

3-3. If N is a 3-digit number whose units' digit is 3 (and whose hundreds' digit is not 0), what is the probability that N is divisible by 3?

3-3.

3-4. What are the 4 ordered pairs of real numbers (x,y) which simultaneously satisfy the system

$$x + xy + y = 11 \quad \text{and} \quad x^2y + xy^2 = 30?$$

3-4.

3-5. In a river with a steady current, it takes the Bionic Woman 6 minutes to swim a certain distance upstream, but it takes her only 3 minutes to swim back. How many minutes would it take a doll of the Bionic Woman to float this same distance downstream?

3-5.

3-6. In the coordinate plane, what is the area of the region common to $x \geq 0$, $y \leq 1$, and $x^2 + y^2 \leq 4y$?

3-6.

Contest Number 4   **February 7, 1978**

Name _____ Grade Level _____ Score _____

Time Limit: 30 minutes   *Answer Column*

4-1.   A man born in the year x^2 died, on his 87th birthday, in the year $(x + 1)^2$. In what year was he born?

4-1.

4-2.   What is the simplified numerical value of the quotient

$$\frac{\sin 10° \; \cos 10° \; \tan 10° \; \cot 10° \; \sec 10° \; \csc 10°}{\sin 20° \; \cos 20° \; \tan 20° \; \cot 20° \; \sec 20° \; \csc 20°} \; ?$$

4-2.

4-3.   What are all two-digit positive integers in which the difference between the integer and the product of its two digits is 12?

4-3.

4-4.   In an isosceles triangle, the perpendicular bisector of one leg passes through the midpoint of the base. If the length of this leg is 10, how long is the base?

4-4.

4-5.   Semicircles drawn on each side of a triangle have areas of 9π, 16π, and 25π. What is the area of the triangle?

4-5.

4-6.   In the coordinate plane, the graphs of the equations

$$x^2 + y^2 - 4x + 6y - 12 = 0 \quad \text{and} \quad y = ax^2 + bx + c$$

have exactly 3 points in common. Two of these points are (–3,–3) and (7,–3). What are all possible coordinates of the third point?

4-6.

© 1978 by Mathematics Leagues Inc.

HIGH SCHOOL MATHEMATICS CONTESTS

P.O. Box 720, Tenafly, New Jersey 07670

Contest Number 5   **March 7, 1978**

Name _____ Grade Level _____ Score _____

Time Limit: 30 minutes   *Answer Column*

5-1.   A series of 7 books was published at 9-year intervals. When the 7th book was published, the sum of the publication years was 13601. In what year was the 4th book published?

5-1.

5-2.   One altitude of an equilateral triangle is a side of one square, and one side of the same equilateral triangle is a side of a second square. The area of the larger of these squares is 56. What is the area of the smaller of these squares?

5-2.

5-3.   What are all values of x which satisfy $4^{x^3 + 5x^2 - 6x} = 1$?

5-3.

5-4.   What is the degree-measure of the least positive angle x for which

$$\log_2 \cos x = -\frac{1}{2}?$$

5-4.

5-5.   For all positive numbers a and b, a function f satisfies the equation $f(ab) = f(a) + f(b)$. If $f(2) = x$ and $f(5) = y$, what is the value of $f(100)$, in terms of x and y?

5-5.

5-6.   Let z be a complex number and $\bar{z}$ be its conjugate. What are the four values of z for which $z\bar{z} = 5$ and $z^2 + \bar{z}^2 = 6$?

5-6.

Contest Number 6   April 11, 1978

Name _____ **Grade Level** _____ **Score** _____

Time Limit: 30 minutes   *Answer Column*

6-1. On the planet Oberon, there are as many days in a week as there are weeks in a month. The number of months in an Oberon year is twice the number of days in a month. If there are 1250 days in an Oberon year, how many months are there in an Oberon year?

6-1.

6-2. Regular hexagon *ABCDEF* has side $\overline{AF}$ in common with regular hexagon *AFGHIJ* and side $\overline{BC}$ in common with regular hexagon *BCKLMN*. All three hexagons are coplanar and nonoverlapping. If $AB = 64$, what is the value of *JN*?

6-2.

6-3. In degrees, what is the measure of the least positive angle x for which

$$\left(2^{\sin^2 x}\right)\left(2^{\cos^2 x}\right)\left(2^{\tan^2 x}\right) = 2^2?$$

6-3.

6-4. If $b = \log_3 x$, what is the real value of x which satisfies

$$\log_b\left(\log_3 x^2\right) = 2?$$

6-4.

6-5. The lengths of the sides of a triangle are 25, 29, and 36. There is a point on the longest side of the triangle whose distance from the opposite vertex is 20. What is the distance from this point to the midpoint of the shortest side?

6-5.

6-6. All the positive integers with an initial digit of 2 are written down in succession. What is the 1978th digit thus written?

6-6.

Solutions on Page 39 • Answers on Page 66   7

Contest Number 1   October 24, 1978

Name _____ Grade Level _____ Score _____

Time Limit: 30 minutes   *Answer Column*

1-1.   The sum of ten positive odd numbers is 20. What is the largest number which can be used as an addend in this sum?

1-1.

1-2.   After a period of particularly bad weather, the Parliament of Franistan decreed that there would no longer be any weather on even-numbered calendar dates. During one of the months following that decree, three Mondays had no weather! On what day of the week did the 13th of that month occur?

1-2.

1-3.   For how many of the first 100 positive integers x does

$$(6x^2 - 13x + 6)(4x + 3) = (8x^2 - 6x - 9)(3x - 2)?$$

1-3.

1-4.   In the diagram, congruent radii $\overline{AB}$ and $\overline{CD}$ intersect tangent $\overline{BC}$. If the shaded regions have equal areas, and if $AB = 1$, what is the area of quadrilateral $ABCD$?

1-4.

1-5.   In the coordinate plane, a circle which passes through $(-2,-3)$ and $(2,5)$ cannot also pass through $(1978,y)$. What is the value of y?

1-5.

1-6.   Determine, in simplest form, the numerical value of

$$\sqrt[3]{7 - \sqrt{50}} + \sqrt[3]{7 + \sqrt{50}}.$$

1-6.

HIGH SCHOOL MATHEMATICS CONTESTS

P.O. Box 720, Tenafly, New Jersey 07670

Contest Number 2   **December 5, 1978**

Name _____ Grade Level _____ Score _____

Time Limit: 30 minutes   *Answer Column*

2-1. For all positive integers n, the symbol $n!$ denotes the product of the first n positive integers. Find the value of n for which

$$(3!)(5!)(7!) = n!.$$

2-1.

2-2. A line segment with endpoints $A(2,-2)$ and $B(14,4)$ is extended, through B, to point C. If $BC = \frac{1}{4}AB$, what are the coordinates of point C?

2-2.

2-3. Once upon a time, there lived a worm with two mouths, one at each end. Both mouths ate at the same rate, with equal efficiency. Thirty minutes after the worm began eating a leaf with one mouth, its other mouth joined in the feast. Thirty minutes later, the leaf was completely consumed. If both mouths had been eating at the start, and if one mouth had stopped when half the leaf was eaten, it would have taken the other mouth x minutes to finish the second half. What is the value of x?

2-3.

2-4. What are the 4 values of x for which $(x^2 - 6x + 4)^2 = 16$?

2-4.

2-5. Both legs of an isosceles triangle are radii of a circle, and the length of each radius is 6. The distance from the center of the circle to a point P on the base of the triangle is 4. If the distances from P to the triangle's other vertices are 5 and x, what is the value of x?

2-5.

2-6. What are all ordered pairs of real numbers (x,y) for which

$$17x^2 - 10xy + 2y^2 - 6x + 2 = 0?$$

2-6.

Solutions on Page 41 • Answers on Page 66

9

Contest Number 3   **January 16, 1979**

Name _____ Grade Level _____ Score _____

Time Limit: 30 minutes   *Answer Column*

3-1. Two vertices of an equilateral triangle lie on a diameter a circle whose area is 36π, and the third vertex lies on the circle. What is the largest possible area of the triangle?	3-1.
3-2. Set A has 12 more subsets than set B. How many elements are there in set A?	3-2.
3-3. In a numeration system with a positive integral base, the numerals 104 and 241 represent the degree-measures of a pair of supplementary angles. What is the base of this numeration system?	3-3.
3-4. The numerals $0.AAAAA\ldots$ and $0.BBBBB\ldots$ are repeating decimals whose digits are A and B respectively. What are all ordered pairs of positive integers (A,B) for which $$\sqrt{0.AAAAA\ldots} = 0.BBBBB\ldots\,?$$	3-4.
3-5. A man was doodling randomly on a tic-tac-toe board. What is the probability that the first three boxes in which he doodled corresponded to a winning path?	3-5.
3-6. For how many integers $c \leq 50$ will the solutions of the equation $x^2 - 4x + c = 0$ be complex conjugates of the form $a \pm bi$, where a and b are positive integers and i is the imaginary unit?	3-6.

Contest Number 4   **February 13, 1979**

Name _____ Grade Level _____ Score _____

Time Limit: 30 minutes   *Answer Column*

4-1.   In a subtraction example, the four-digit number 48*NN* is subtracted from the four-digit number 197*N*, where the *N*'s represent hidden digits (not necessarily identical). What is the greatest possible result obtainable?

4-1.

4-2.   In the coordinate plane, the graph of the function *f* is the single point (3,–4). What is the distance between the graph of *f* and the graph of its inverse, f^{-1}?

4-2.

4-3.   What are the 4 ordered pairs of integers (*x,y*) for which

$$(x + 2y)(2x + y) = 27?$$

4-3.

4-4.   If $0° \leq x \leq 180°$, find, in degrees, all angles *x* which satisfy

$$(0.2)^{\cos x} < 1.$$

4-4.

4-5.   In a trapezoid, the lengths of the bases are 4 and 16, and the lower base angles are 30° and 60°. What is the distance between the midpoints of the two bases?

4-5.

4-6.   If eggs had cost *x*¢ less per dozen, it would have cost 3¢ less for *x* + 3 eggs than if they had cost *x*¢ more per dozen. What is *x*?

4-6.

Solutions on Page 43 • Answers on Page 66

HIGH SCHOOL MATHEMATICS CONTESTS

P.O. Box 720, Tenafly, New Jersey 07670

Contest Number 5   **March 13, 1979**

Name _____ Grade Level _____ Score _____

Time Limit: 30 minutes   *Answer Column*

5-1.   Four congruent chords are perpen-
       dicular to a line through the centers
       of externally tangent congruent cir-
       cles, as shown. The distance between
       the two furthest chords is 20, and
       the distance between two chords of
       the same circle is 8. What is the area
       of one of the circles?

5-1.

5-2.   At the College of Hard Knocks, 99% of the 100 students are girls,
       but only 98% of the students living on campus are girls. If some
       girls live on campus, how many students live off campus?

5-2.

5-3.   In the series $20^2 - 19^2 + 18^2 - 17^2 + \ldots + 2^2 - 1^2$, the signs alter-
       nate between squares of consecutive integers. What is the sum of
       this series?

5-3.

5-4.   What is the least possible distance between the graphs of the equa-
       tions $x^2 + y^2 = 1$ and $(x - 5)^2 + (y - 12)^2 = 1$?

5-4.

5-5.   The sides of a triangle have lengths $\log_2 3$, $\log_2 7$, and $\log_2 x$. What
       is the least possible integral value of x?

5-5.

5-6.   The number 90^9 has 1900 different positive integral divisors. How
       many of these are squares of integers?

5-6.

© 1979 by Mathematics Leagues Inc.

Contest Number 6   **April 10, 1979**

Name _____ Grade Level _____ Score _____

Time Limit: 30 minutes   *Answer Column*

6-1. What is the least positive integer that can be added to the product of any four consecutive integers so that the result is always the square of an integer?

6-1.

6-2. Which is larger, $\sqrt[3]{\frac{1}{2}}$ or $\sqrt{\frac{1}{3}}$?

6-2.

6-3. What is the degree-measure of the acute angle formed by extending sides $\overline{AB}$ and $\overline{ED}$ of regular nine-sided polygon *ABCDEFGHI* until these extensions meet?

6-3.

6-4. If $\sin^2(\frac{\pi}{9}) + \sin^2(\frac{2\pi}{9}) + \sin^2(\frac{3\pi}{9}) + \sin^2(\frac{4\pi}{9}) = \frac{9}{4}$, evaluate

$$\cos^2(\tfrac{\pi}{9}) + \cos^2(\tfrac{2\pi}{9}) + \cos^2(\tfrac{3\pi}{9}) + \cos^2(\tfrac{4\pi}{9}).$$

6-4.

6-5. What are all ordered triples of numbers (x,y,z) for which

$$x + y + z = 6,\ x(y + z) = 5,\ \text{and}\ y(x + z) = 8?$$

6-5.

6-6. Two gamblers each have a deck of 99 cards, numbered from 1 to 99. Each randomly selects one card from his deck. The numbers on these two cards are then multiplied together, and the first gambler pays the second a dollar amount equal to this product. For this to be a fair game, how many dollars should the second gambler pay the first for the privilege of playing this game once?

6-6.

© 1979 by Mathematics Leagues Inc.

Contest Number 1   **October 23, 1979**

Name _____ Grade Level _____ Score _____

Time Limit: 30 minutes   *Answer Column*

1-1. Two 5×5 squares overlap to form a 5×7 rectangle, as shown. What is the area of the region in which the two squares overlap?

1-1.

1-2. What is the least integer x for which $\dfrac{12}{x+1}$ represents an integer?

1-2.

1-3. Giving your answer in simplest form, what is the value of
$$(987654321)(987654321) - (987654323)(987654319)?$$

1-3.

1-4. What are all ordered pairs of real numbers (x,y) for which
$$\sqrt{x} + \sqrt{y} = 17 \text{ and } x - y = 85?$$

1-4.

1-5. What is the ordered pair of numbers (a,b) for which $x-3$ is a factor of both
$$x^2 - (a + b)x + 3b \text{ and } (a - 1)x^2 + bx + a?$$

1-5.

1-6. A fuel tank receives a continuous, steady flow of 2000 liters per hour. The tank experiences a steady rate of fuel usage within each of the 6 consecutive 4-hour periods every day. Every day, usage during these periods is, respectively, 6000, 13500, 7300, 10000, 8000, and 3200 liters. What is the capacity, in liters, of the smallest tank which could ensure there would always be at least 200 liters of fuel in the tank?

1-6.

Contest Number 2   **November 20, 1979**

Name _____ Grade Level _____ Score _____

Time Limit: 30 minutes   *Answer Column*

2-1. On five tests (on which the scores could range anywhere from 0 through 100), Johnny had an average of exactly 88. What is the lowest score Johnny could have received on one of these tests?

2-1.

2-2. What are all real values of x for which $5^x + 12^x = 13^x$?

2-2.

2-3. What is the ordered pair of real numbers (x,y) which satisfies
$$|x + y + 7| + |2x - y + 2| = 0?$$

2-3.

2-4. If a, b, c, and d are real numbers, what is the numerical value of the sum $a + b + c + d$ when $3x^3 - 8x^2 + 7$ is written in the form
$$a(x - 2)^3 + b(x - 2)^2 + c(x - 2) + d?$$

2-4.

2-5. The squash season is nearing its end, and the current individual standings are shown in the chart. Each of the 8 players must still play 28 games, 4 with each of the other players. How many players still have a theoretical chance to at least tie for the championship?

Player:	A	B	C	D	E	F	G	H
Games Won:	92	91	90	71	67	66	44	39
Games Lost:	48	49	50	69	73	74	96	101

2-5.

2-6. From a point interior to a regular hexagon, perpendiculars drawn to the sides of the hexagon have lengths, in size order, of 3, 6, $7\frac{1}{2}$, $13\frac{1}{2}$, 15, and 18. How long is a side of this hexagon?

2-6.

HIGH SCHOOL MATHEMATICS CONTESTS

P.O. Box 720, Tenafly, New Jersey 07670

Contest Number 3   **December 18, 1979**

Name _____ Grade Level _____ Score _____

Time Limit: 30 minutes   *Answer Column*

3-1. What is the sum of all the integers from –100 to 100?   3-1. _____

3-2. One stamp is randomly selected from a 10×10 sheet of 100 stamps. What is the probability that the stamp selected was *not* one of the sheet's border stamps?   3-2. _____

3-3. In how many different ways can 35¢ be made up of coins of the types currently being minted in this country?   3-3. _____

3-4. Triangle ABC is inscribed in a circle. If $\overline{AC}$ is a side of a 21-sided inscribed regular polygon, $\overline{AB}$ a side of a 28-sided inscribed regular polygon, and $\overline{BC}$ a side of an n-sided inscribed regular polygon, what is the larger of the two possible values of n?   3-4. _____

3-5. What is the real value of x which satisfies

$$(\log_x 2x)(\log_{10} x) = 3?$$ 3-5. _____

3-6. If $x = y^2$ and $y = x^2$, what is the least possible real value of

$$x^2 + x + 1,$$

where x and y are complex numbers?   3-6. _____

HIGH SCHOOL MATHEMATICS CONTESTS

P.O. Box 720, Tenafly, New Jersey 07670

Contest Number 4

January 15, 1980

Name _____ Grade Level _____ Score _____

Time Limit: 30 minutes

Answer Column

4-1. Starting with 1, at most how many consecutive positive integers can be added together *before* the sum exceeds 200?

4-1.

4-2. If a and b are not equal, and if $ax = bx$, what is the numerical value of $3(a - b)^x$?

4-2.

4-3. If $\tan x + \cot x = \dfrac{144}{25}$, what is the numerical value of

$$\frac{1}{\tan x} + \frac{1}{\cot x}?$$

4-3.

4-4. A lattice point in the plane is a point both of whose coordinates are integers. How many lattice points are on the graph of

$$y = x\sqrt{2} - 1?$$

4-4.

4-5. An American family, driving along a highway at a legal speed, noted that their car's odometer reading was 45954 miles, a palindrome (which reads the same forwards or backwards). Two hours later, the odometer displayed yet another palindrome! Determine, in miles per hour, the car's speed during that two-hour period.

4-5.

4-6. In the diagram, M is the midpoint of $\overline{AC}$, and $\overline{PM}$ is parallel to $\overline{BQ}$. The area of $\triangle ABC$ is 100, while the area of $\triangle APM$ is 36. What is the area of $\triangle MPQ$?

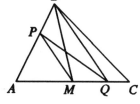

4-6.

Solutions on Page 49 • Answers on Page 66

Contest Number 5   **February 12, 1980**

Name _____ Grade Level _____ Score _____

Time Limit: 30 minutes   *Answer Column*

5-1.   Three concentric circles have radii of lengths 5, 12, and 13. What is   5-1.
       the length of the shortest line segment which could contain 1 point
       on each of the 3 circles?

5-2.   If I have 2 more brothers than sisters, and each of my brothers also   5-2.
       has 2 more brothers than sisters, how many more brothers than
       sisters does my oldest sister have?

5-3.   If i is the imaginary unit, what is the *decimal* equivalent of   5-3.

       $$\left(\frac{4}{5}\right)^{i^{434}} ?$$

5-4.   What are all values of x which satisfy $\left(5 - \frac{1}{x}\right) = \sqrt{5 - \frac{1}{x}}$?   5-4.

5-5.   The lengths of the sides of a triangle are 2, 3, and x, and the area   5-5.
       of the triangle is also x. What is the value of x?

5-6.   What is the ordered pair of numbers (x,y) which satisfies   5-6.

       $$(x^a)(y^b) = \left(\frac{3}{4}\right)^{a-b} \quad \text{and} \quad (x^b)(y^a) = \left(\frac{3}{4}\right)^{b-a}$$

       for all real numbers a and b?

Contest Number 6   March 25, 1980

Name _____ Grade Level _____ Score _____

Time Limit: 30 minutes   *Answer Column*

6-1. I have twice as many nickels as dimes. If the value of my nickels is $5.00, what is the value of my dimes?

6-1.

6-2. The values of a, b, c, and d are 1, 2, 3, and 4, but *not* necessarily in that order. What is the largest possible value of

$$ab + bc + cd + da?$$

6-2.

6-3. The lengths of the sides of a non-isosceles triangle, in size order, are 5, x, and 15. What are all possible integral values of x?

6-3.

6-4. [In this problem, use the fact that 1 ton = 2000 lbs. and 1 mile = 5280 feet.] An elephant weighing 2.64 tons and a rabbit weighing 1 lb. are balanced on a very long, perfectly rigid teeterboard (see-saw). If the elephant starts sliding toward the fulcrum at the uniform rate of 1 foot per minute, how many *miles per hour* must the rabbit run in order to maintain balance?

6-4.

6-5. What is the product of the first 10 terms of a geometric series whose 1st term is 1 and whose 10th term is 2?

6-5.

6-6. In $\triangle ABC$, what is the ordered pair of real numbers (x,y) for which $\sin A : \sin B : \sin C = 4:5:6$, but $\cos A : \cos B : \cos C = x:y:2$?

6-6.

Solutions on Page 51 • Answers on Page 66

19

HIGH SCHOOL MATHEMATICS CONTESTS

P.O. Box 720, Tenafly, New Jersey 07670

Contest Number 1   October 21, 1980

Name _____ Grade Level _____ Score _____

Time Limit: 30 minutes   *Answer Column*

1-1. If $\left(\frac{2}{3}\right)\left(\frac{3}{4}\right)\left(\frac{4}{5}\right)\left(\frac{5}{6}\right)\left(\frac{6}{7}\right)\left(\frac{7}{8}\right)\left(\frac{8}{9}\right)\left(\frac{9}{10}\right)\left(\frac{10}{11}\right)\left(\frac{11}{12}\right) = \frac{1}{n}$, find n.   1-1.

1-2. What is the value of k for which $\frac{k-1}{k+1}$ and $\frac{k+1}{k-1}$ are both integers?   1-2.

1-3. What is the positive number x for which

$$\sqrt{x} = \sqrt[3]{y} \quad \text{and} \quad \sqrt{y} = 8?$$ 1-3.

1-4. What is the ordered pair of real numbers (x,y) for which   1-4.

$$123x + 321y = 345 \text{ and}$$
$$321x + 123y = 543?$$

1-5. The costs to a concessionaire at a ball game are partly fixed and partly vary directly with the number of people in attendance. If 4000 people attend the game, the concessionaire's costs will be $1300. If 2800 people attend, his costs will be $970. What are his costs, in dollars, if only 1000 people attend?   1-5.

1-6. Four coplanar regular convex polygons share a common vertex but have no interior points in common. Each polygon is adjacent to two of the other polygons, and each pair of adjacent polygons has a common side of length 1. What are all possible perimeters of such a configuration?   1-6.

HIGH SCHOOL MATHEMATICS CONTESTS

P.O. Box 720, Tenafly, New Jersey 07670

Contest Number 2   **November 18, 1980**

Name _____ Grade Level _____ Score _____

Time Limit: 30 minutes   *Answer Column*

2-1. What is the difference between the sum of the first 20 positive even integers and the sum of the first 20 positive odd integers? That is, what is the value of

$$(2 + 4 + 6 + \ldots + 40) - (1 + 3 + 5 + \ldots + 39)?$$

2-1.

2-2. Which is greater—the perimeter of

the shaded region or the perimeter of

one of the rectangles? (Write "S" for

shaded region or "R" for rectangle.)

2-2.

2-3. What are the four real values of x for which

$$\left|(2 - |x|)\right| = 1?$$

2-3.

2-4. If $3 \leq y \leq 22$, for how many ordered pairs of positive integers (x,y) does y exceed x by at least 2?

2-4.

2-5. Only four integers between 100 and 1000 equal the sum of the cubes of their digits. Three of these are 153, 370, and 407. What is the fourth?

2-5.

2-6. What is the least value of k for which the inequality

$$k < \frac{2x - 7}{2x^2 - 2x - 5} < 1$$

has no real solution?

2-6.

Contest Number 3   **December 16, 1980**

Name _____ Grade Level _____ Score _____

Time Limit: 30 minutes	*Answer Column*
3-1. There are two different ways to put the digits 1, 2, 3, 4, and 5 into the blanks between the parentheses, one digit per blank, so that $$\frac{(\ )\times(\ )}{(\ )} = (\ ) + (\ )$$ is a true statement. What are these *two* ways? [NOTE: Changes in order only are *not* considered different.]	3-1.
3-2. The interiors of all of the unit squares of an 8 by 8 checkerboard are to be colored with crayon. Any two such squares having a side or a vertex in common will be colored with a different crayon. What is the least number of different crayons needed?	3-2.
3-3. What is the ordered pair of real numbers (x,y) which does satisfy $y = 5x - 15$, but which does *not* satisfy $\frac{y}{x-3} = 5$?	3-3.
3-4. On an 8×15 rectangle, congruent triangles ABC and $A'B'C'$ are drawn as illustrated, with corresponding sides parallel. If $AB = 7$, $AC = 8$, and $BC = 9$, what is the value of AA'?	3-4.
3-5. What are all values of x for which $(x^2-5x+5)^{x^2-9x+20} = 1$?	3-5.
3-6. What is the least positive integral value of n for which $\frac{n-12}{5n+23}$ is a non-zero reducible fraction?	3-6.

HIGH SCHOOL MATHEMATICS CONTESTS

P.O. Box 720, Tenafly, New Jersey 07670

Contest Number 4   January 13, 1981

Name _____ Grade Level _____ Score _____

Time Limit: 30 minutes   *Answer Column*

4-1. The lengths of the sides of a triangle are 3, 4, and 6. What is the least possible perimeter of a similar triangle one of whose sides has a length of 12?	4-1.
4-2. Increasing $100 by a certain percent produces the same result as decreasing $300 by the same percent. What is this percent?	4-2.
4-3. Alice has 3 pennies, 3 nickels, and 3 dimes. How many different amounts of money can Alice make using one or more of these 9 coins?	4-3.
4-4. If i represents the imaginary unit, what is the ordered pair of real numbers (x,y) for which $$x + xi + y - yi = -1 + 7i?$$	4-4.
4-5. For every real number k, let $[k]$ represent the greatest integer less than or equal to k. In the coordinate plane, what is the area of the region which represents $$[x]^2 + [y]^2 = 1?$$	4-5.
4-6. The solutions of $x^3 - 2x^2 + 3x + 4 = 0$ are a, b, and c. What is the numerical value of $(a + b)(a + c)(b + c)$?	4-6.

Contest Number 5   **February 10, 1981**

Name _____ Grade Level _____ Score _____

Time Limit: 30 minutes	*Answer Column*
5-1. The product of the repeating decimals 0.333 . . . and 0.666 . . . is the repeating decimal 0.*NNN* . . . . What is the digit *N*?	5-1.
5-2. What is the difference between the sum of all eight positive integral divisors of 66 and the sum of all eight positive integral divisors of 70?	5-2.
5-3. A lattice point in the plane is a point both of whose coordinates are integers. If endpoints are included, how many lattice points lie on the line segment joining (0,0) and (100,150)?	5-3.
5-4. What are both real values of *x* which satisfy the equation $$\left(\frac{2x+3}{3x+2}\right)^2 + \left(\frac{2x+3}{3x+2}\right) = 6?$$	5-4.
5-5. If $\log_{10} 25 = 1.39794$, what is the number of digits in the complete expansion of 25^{100}?	5-5.
5-6. The lengths of the legs of a right triangle are 3 and 4. Two congruent circles, externally tangent to each other, are drawn inside the triangle, with each circle tangent to the hypotenuse and one of the legs. What is the distance between the centers of the two circles?	5-6.

HIGH SCHOOL MATHEMATICS CONTESTS

P.O. Box 720, Tenafly, New Jersey 07670

Contest Number 6   **March 24, 1981**

Name _____ Grade Level _____ Score _____

Time Limit: 30 minutes | *Answer Column*

6-1.   For every 2 widgets I buy at the regular price, I get a 3rd widget for a penny. I spent 45¢ for 9 widgets. In cents, what is the regular price of 1 widget? | 6-1.

6-2.   What is the simplest expression for $\dfrac{2^{40}}{4^{20}}$? | 6-2.

6-3.   Let a, b, and c be integers whose square roots are the lengths of the sides of a right triangle. What is the least possible value of the sum $a + b + c$? | 6-3.

6-4.   What are all real values of x which satisfy the equation
$$(x - 3)(x^2 + 4x + 4) = (x - 3)?$$ | 6-4.

6-5.   If $x < y$, find the ordered pair of real numbers (x,y) which satisfies
$$x^3 + y^3 = 400 \quad \text{and} \quad x^2y + xy^2 = 200.$$ | 6-5.

6-6.   Find the perimeters of all non-congruent triangles in which the lengths of all three sides are integral, the cosine of one angle is $-\frac{1}{4}$, and the length of one of the two sides *not* opposite this angle is 16. | 6-6.

Solutions on Page 57 • Answers on Page 67

25

HIGH SCHOOL MATHEMATICS CONTESTS

P.O. Box 720, Tenafly, New Jersey 07670

Contest Number 1   October 27, 1981

Name _____ Grade Level _____ Score _____

Time Limit: 30 minutes   *Answer Column*

1-1. What is the ordered pair of integers (a,b) for which $(x+a)(x+3) = x^2+bx-15$ for all values of x?

1-1.

1-2. Nine congruent rectangles are placed as shown to form a large rectangle whose area is 180. What is the perimeter of the large rectangle?

1-2.

1-3. What are the two values of x which satisfy $\frac{2}{x} + \frac{x}{2} = \frac{3}{x} + \frac{x}{3}$?

1-3.

1-4. How many integers greater than 4 million and less than 9 million are perfect squares?

1-4.

1-5. Into a box are put ten smaller boxes. Each of these smaller boxes is either left empty or is filled with ten still smaller empty boxes. Of all the boxes, exactly six have other boxes inserted into them. Of all the boxes, how many remain empty?

1-5.

1-6. The coordinates of the vertices of quadrilateral $ABCD$ are $A(-8,12)$, $B(7,15)$, $C(13,-9)$ and $D(-2,-3)$. Find the coordinates of the centroid (center of gravity) of the region bounded by this quadrilateral.

1-6.

Contest Number 2   November 24, 1981

Name _____ Grade Level _____ Score _____

Time Limit: 30 minutes   *Answer Column*

2-1. At the bank, Al exchanged a $10 bill for an equal number of nickels, dimes, and quarters. How many of each type of coin did Al receive?

2-1.

2-2. In the accompanying diagram, $AE = 3$, $DE = 4$, and $AD = 5$. What is the area of rectangle $ABCD$?

2-2.

2-3. There is a set of 1981 different integers. The sum of all of these integers is 1982. At *most*, how many of the integers in this set can be odd?

2-3.

2-4. How many integral values of x satisfy the inequality
$$8 < |3x + 4| < 32?$$

2-4.

2-5. What is the ordered pair of real numbers (x,y) for which
$$16^x - 16^y = 192 \quad \text{and} \quad 4^x - 4^y = 8?$$

2-5.

2-6. A sphere is inscribed in a regular tetrahedron. If the length of an altitude of the tetrahedron is 36, what is the length of a radius of the sphere?

2-6.

Contest Number 3   **January 5, 1982**

Name _____ Grade Level _____ Score _____

Time Limit: 30 minutes   *Answer Column*

3-1. The integers M and N have no digits in common, even though each of their digits is a digit of the integer 1982. If no digit is used more than once, find the largest possible value of the product MN.

3-1.

3-2. The area of square I is 1. A diagonal of square I is a side of square II, a diagonal of square II is a side of square III, and a diagonal of square III is a side of square IV. What is the area of square IV?

3-2.

3-3. If $\dfrac{14x - 3y}{x + 2y} = 4$, what is the numerical value of $\dfrac{x+y}{x-y}$?

3-3.

3-4. If $3^x = 5$, what is the value of 3^{2x+3}?

3-4.

3-5. Amarillo Slim and Jimmy the Greek alternately draw cards from a (face down) deck of ordinary playing cards. Slim draws first, and his first draw is the ace of diamonds. If they continue drawing alternately, what is the probability that Slim will also be the one to draw the ace of spades?

3-5.

3-6. What are all rational numbers x which satisfy the equation

$$\frac{x + \sqrt{x}}{x - \sqrt{x}} = \frac{81x(x-1)}{4}?$$

3-6.

Contest Number 4   **February 2, 1982**

Name _____ Grade Level _____ Score _____

Time Limit: 30 minutes   *Answer Column*

4-1.   The square of the nine-digit number 111 111 111 is an *n*-digit number. What is the value of *n*?

4-1.

4-2.   If $a \uparrow b$ means a^b, and if $a \downarrow b$ means $\sqrt[b]{a}$, what is the value of

$$[(2 \uparrow 6) \downarrow 3] \uparrow 2?$$

4-2.

4-3.   In right $\triangle ABC$, what is the numerical value of

$$\sin^2 A + \sin^2 B + \sin^2 C?$$

4-3.

4-4.   In the diagram shown, *ABCDE* is a regular pentagon, and $\triangle APE$ is equilateral. What is the measure of obtuse angle *BPD*?

4-4.

4-5.   In an arithmetic progression, the 25th term is 2552 and the 52nd term is 5279. What is the 79th term?

4-5.

4-6.   A circle is centered at the vertex of the right angle of an isosceles right triangle. The circle passes through both trisection points of the hypotenuse of the triangle. If the length of a radius of the circle is 10, what is the area of the triangle?

4-6.

HIGH SCHOOL MATHEMATICS CONTESTS

P.O. Box 720, Tenafly, New Jersey 07670

Contest Number 5   **March 16, 1982**

Name _____ Grade Level _____ Score _____

Time Limit: 30 minutes   *Answer Column*

5-1. Express as a fraction in simplest form: 5-1.

$$\frac{3+6+\ 9+12+\ldots+291+294}{4+8+12+16+\ldots+388+392}.$$

5-2. Two congruent circles are externally tangent. A   5-2.

segment connects the center of one circle to the

point where the segment is tangent to the other

circle. The length of this segment is 12. What is

the length of a radius of one of these two circles?

5-3. If $3^{33} + 3^{33} + 3^{33} = 3^x$, what is the value of x?   5-3.

5-4. What is the simplified numerical value of the product   5-4.

$(\tan 15°)(\tan 30°)(\tan 45°)(\tan 60°)(\tan 75°)$?

5-5. Consider the following 2 sets of consecutive integers: $\{10, \ldots ,20\}$ 5-5.
and $\{21, \ldots ,30\}$. Each element of the 1st set is multiplied, in turn,
by each element of the 2nd set. Find the sum of all these products.

5-6. What is the numerical coefficient of x^2 in the complete expansion   5-6.
of $(x^2 + 5x + 2)^5(x^2 - 7x + 3)^9$?

Solutions on Page 62 • Answers on Page 67

Contest Number 6   April 20, 1982

Name _____ Grade Level _____ Score _____

Time Limit: 30 minutes   *Answer Column*

6-1. What is the average of the first 50 positive integers?	6-1.
6-2. What is the value of x which satisfies $(3^x)(4^x) = 5^x$?	6-2.
6-3. What is the value of x which satisfies $\sqrt[3]{x\sqrt{x}} = 4$?	6-3.
6-4. The area of square *ABCD* is 1. As illustrated at the right, diagonal $\overline{AC}$ is extended its own length to point *E*. How long is $\overline{BE}$?	6-4.
6-5. On a plane, two men together had 135 kilograms of luggage. The first paid \$1.35 for his excess luggage and the second paid \$2.70 for his excess luggage. Had all the luggage belonged to one person, the excess luggage charge would have been \$8.10. At most how many kilograms of luggage is each person permitted to bring on the plane free of additional charge?	6-5.
6-6. A certain parabola passes through the points (5,1) and (13,–7) and has the *y*-axis as its directrix. What are the coordinates of all points at which the vertex of this parabola could be located?	6-6.

The Complete Solutions
November, 1977 – April, 1982

Problem 1-1

Let t be the number of tentacles a Martian has. Since $IQ = kt^2$, $75 = k(5^2)$, so $k = 3$. For a Martian with 8 tentacles, $IQ = k(8^2) = 3(64) = \boxed{192}$.

Problem 1-2

To meet the conditions of the problem, every line should intersect every other line. When 5 lines are drawn, the number of regions into which the plane is partitioned is $\boxed{16}$.

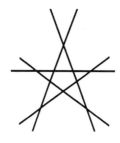

Problem 1-3

If a radius of the smaller circle is r and a radius of the larger circle is R, then the area of the trapezoid $= \frac{1}{2}h(b_1 + b_2) = \frac{1}{2}(r + R) \times (2r+2R) = (r+R)^2 = 8^2 = \boxed{64}$.

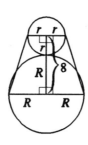

Problem 1-4

In base ten, $\frac{1}{n}$ will terminate if and only if n's only factors are 2's and/or 5's (factors of the base). For example, $\frac{1}{40}$ will terminate since $40 = 2 \times 2 \times 2 \times 5$. Similarly, the fraction $\frac{1}{n}$ will terminate, when written in base b, if and only if the factors of n are all factors of b. Since $51 = 3 \times 17$, n's factors must be 3's or 17's. Since $187 = 11 \times 17$, n's factors must be 11's or 17's. Clearly, the least n is $\boxed{17}$.

Problem 1-5

Regrouping and completing cubes, $(x^3 - 3x^2 + 3x - 1) + (y^3 + 6y^2 + 12y + 8) = 1$, or $(x-1)^3 + (y+2)^3 = 1$. Since x and y are both integers, either $(x-1) = 1$ and $(y+2) = 0$, or $(x-1) = 0$ and $(y+2) = 1$. Therefore, $(x,y) = \boxed{(2,-2), (1,-1)}$.

[We'll prove the assertion of the second sentence: if $a^3 + b^3 = 1$, then $ab = 0$. Factoring, if $a^3 + b^3 = 1$, we get $(a+b)(a^2 - ab + b^2) = 1$. Since a and b are both integers, either both factors are 1 or both factors are -1. Solving the resulting equations, $a = 0$ or $b = 0$.]

Problem 1-6

Using the Pythagorean Theorem, $AE = 3$ and $CF = 12$. Also, $\triangle AED \sim \triangle AHB$, so $3:4 = AH:BH$; and $\triangle CFD \sim \triangle CHB$, so $\frac{CF}{DF} = \frac{12}{5} = \frac{CH}{BH} = \frac{18-AH}{BH} = \frac{18-(3/4)BH}{BH}$. Thus, $BH = \frac{40}{7}$. The area of $\triangle ABC$ is $\frac{1}{2} \times 18 \times \frac{40}{7} = \boxed{\frac{360}{7}}$.

Contests written and compiled by Steven R. Conrad & Daniel Flegler   Mathematics Leagues Inc., © 1977

Problem 2-1

Let t_n denote the nth term. It is given that $t_4 + t_5 = t_6$. It follows that $t_5 = t_6 - t_4 = 6 - 4 = 2$. Then, $t_7 = t_5 + t_6 = 2 + 6 = 8$. Thus, $t_8 = t_6 + t_7 = 6 + 8 = \boxed{14}$.

Problem 2-2

All the bisectors of the angles of any regular polygon meet at the center of that polygon's circumscribed circle. The length of $\overline{AP}$ is the length of a radius of the circumcircle, which is $\boxed{14}$.

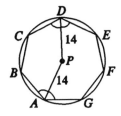

Problem 2-3

There is $\frac{1}{2}$ liter remaining in the first urn after the first pouring. Any time there is $\frac{1}{2}$ liter in the first urn, and $\left(\frac{1}{n}\right)\left(\frac{1}{2}\right)$ liters is added to it, the number of liters then removed will be $\frac{1}{n+1} \times \frac{n+1}{2n} = \frac{1}{2n}$, the amount just added. Therefore, following the 1st pouring, there will always be $\frac{1}{2}$ liter in the first urn after a pouring is made from that urn. The 1977th pouring is made from the first urn, so the number of liters then remaining will be $\boxed{\frac{1}{2}}$.

Problem 2-4

In an n-element set, there are 2^n subsets. If n is the number of elements in A, there are 2^n elements in set B. Therefore, B has 2^{2^n} subsets. Since $2^{2^n} = 16 = 2^{2^2}$, $n = \boxed{2}$.

Problem 2-5

Since x, y, and z are unequal, the original expression has a sum of $\dfrac{x(z-y) + y(x-z) + z(y-x)}{(x-y)(y-z)(z-x)}$. This simplifies to $\dfrac{xz - xy + xy - yz + yz - xz}{(x-y)(y-z)(z-x)} = 0$, so the number of triples is $\boxed{\text{0 or none}}$.

Problem 2-6

Method I: If $AB = a$, then $AP = a$ also. Since $\triangle ABP \sim \triangle PBC$, $BC = \frac{36}{a}$. Since $BC = AD$, $\frac{36}{a} = a + 5$. Consequently, $a^2 + 5a - 36 = (a-4)(a+9) = 0$, and $AB = a = \boxed{4}$.

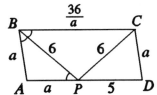

Method II: In $\triangle PDC$, $6^2 = 5^2 + a^2 - 10a \cos D$ and $\cos D = \frac{5^2 + a^2 - 6^2}{10a}$. In $\triangle PAB$, $6^2 = a^2 + a^2 - 2a^2 \cos A$, and $\cos A = \frac{2a^2 - 6^2}{2a^2}$. Since $\angle D$ is supplementary to $\angle A$, $\cos D = -\cos A$, so $\frac{25 + a^2 - 36}{10a} = -\frac{2a^2 - 36}{2a^2}$. Clearing fractions, $a(a-4)(a^2 + 14a + 45) = 0$. This equation has one positive solution, $a = 4$.

Contests written and compiled by Steven R. Conrad & Daniel Flegler   Mathematics Leagues Inc., © 1977

Problem 3-1

Of the 4 congruent triangles in the diagram, the square contains 2 triangles and the trapezoid contains 3 triangles.

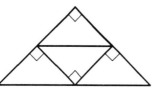

Since the ratio of the area of the trapezoid to the area of the square is 3:2, the area of the trapezoid is $\frac{3}{2} \times 2800 = \boxed{4200}$.

Problem 3-2

Let $y = \sqrt{x}$. Then, $5y^2 + 3y - 2 = (5y - 2)(y + 1) = 0$. Since $y \geq 0$, $y = \frac{2}{5}$, and $x = y^2 = \left(\frac{2}{5}\right)^2 = \boxed{\frac{4}{25}}$.

Problem 3-3

An integer is divisible by 3 if and only if the sum of its digits is divisible by 3. Since the units' digit is 3, we need only consider the probability that the sum of the hundreds' and tens' digits is a multiple of 3. Consider the hundreds' and tens' digits together as comprising a 2-digit number by themselves. There are $99 \div 3 = 33$ numbers from 01 to 99 divisible by 3 and $9 \div 3 = 3$ numbers from 01 to 09 divisible by 3. Thus, of the 90 2-digit numbers, 30 are multiples of 3. Thus, the required probability is $\frac{30}{90} = \boxed{\frac{1}{3}}$.

Problem 3-4

Let $xy = a$ and $x + y = b$. Substituting, $a + b = 11$ and $ab = 30$, so $(a,b) = (5,6)$ or $(6,5)$. Resubstituting, $x + y = 6$ and $xy = 5$, or $x + y = 5$ and $xy = 6$. Solving these two systems independently, the four solutions are $\boxed{(5,1),\ (1,5),\ (2,3),\ (3,2)}$.

Problem 3-5

Let s be the swimming rate of the Bionic Woman in still water, and let c be the rate of the current, both in units per minute. Let d be the distance swum, in units, one way. Since $3(s+c) = d$ and $6(s-c) = d$, subtracting the 2nd equation from twice the 1st yields $12c = d$. Since the doll floats at c units per minute, the required number of minutes is $\boxed{12}$.

Problem 3-6

The 3rd inequality may be rewritten as $x^2 + (y-2)^2 \leq 4$. This represents the circle and its complete interior. The shaded region satisfies all 3 inequalities, and its area is found by subtracting the area of $\triangle OCB$ from the area of sector OAB. Since

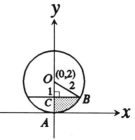

$m\angle AOB = 60°$, this area is $\frac{1}{6} \times \pi \times 2^2 - \frac{1}{2} \times 1 \times \sqrt{3} = \boxed{\frac{2\pi}{3} - \frac{\sqrt{3}}{2}}$.

Contests written and compiled by Steven R. Conrad & Daniel Flegler   Mathematics Leagues Inc., © 1978

Problem 4-1

Since (year of death) − (year of birth) = (age at death), we see that $(x+1)^2 - x^2 = 2x+1 = 87$. Solving, $x = 43$ and his year of birth, x^2, was $\boxed{1849}$.

Problem 4-2

The numerator's value is 1 because the value of each of the products $(\sin 10°)(\csc 10°)$, $(\cos 10°)(\sec 10°)$, and $(\tan 10°)(\cot 10°)$ is 1. Similarly, the value of the denominator is 1, so the value of the fraction is $\boxed{1}$.

Problem 4-3

Let the 2-digit number be $10t+u$. Then, $(10t+u) - tu = 12$. Solving, $t = \frac{12-u}{10-u} = 1 + \frac{2}{10-u}$. Since t is a positive integer if and only if $10-u$ is 2 or 1, the 2 values of u are 8 and 9. The solutions are $\boxed{28, 39}$.

Problem 4-4

A line through the midpoints of two sides of a triangle is parallel to the third side. Therefore, the original triangle is an isosceles right triangle, and its base-length is $\boxed{10\sqrt{2} \text{ or } \sqrt{200}}$.

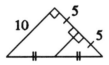

Problem 4-5

Since the areas of the full circles would be 18π, 32π, and 50π, their radii would have respective lengths of $3\sqrt{2}$, $4\sqrt{2}$, $5\sqrt{2}$. The lengths of the sides of the triangle are $6\sqrt{2}$, $8\sqrt{2}$, and $10\sqrt{2}$, so its area is $\frac{1}{2} \times 6\sqrt{2} \times 8\sqrt{2} = \boxed{48}$.

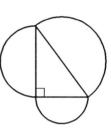

Problem 4-6

In the first equation, after completing the square, we will get $(x-2)^2+(y+3)^2=25$, a circle with center at $(2,-3)$ and radius-length 5. The third point shared by the 2 curves must be an endpoint of the diameter which is perpendicular to the diameter whose endpoints are $(-3,-3)$ and $(7,-3)$. The two possibilities for the coordinates are $\boxed{(2,-8), (2,2)}$.

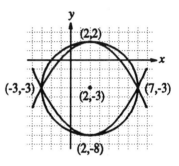

Contests written and compiled by Steven R. Conrad & Daniel Flegler   Mathematics Leagues Inc., © 1978

Problem 5-1

The year of publication of the 4th book is the average of the publication years of all 7 books. This average is $13601 \div 7 =$ $\boxed{1943}$.

Problem 5-2

If two polygons are similar, the ratio of their areas is the square of the ratio of the lengths of two corresponding sides. Let the length of one side of the triangle be 2. Then, by using the ratios of the sides of a $30°-60°-90°$ triangle, an altitude of the equilateral triangle is $\sqrt{3}$. Hence, the ratio $\dfrac{\text{area of the small square}}{\text{area of the large square}} = \left(\dfrac{\sqrt{3}}{2}\right)^2 = \dfrac{3}{4}$.

The area of the larger square is 56. Thus, the area of the smaller square is $\frac{3}{4} \times 56 = \boxed{42}$.

Problem 5-3

Since the right-hand side is 1, the exponent on the left-hand side must be 0. Thus, $0 = x^3 + 5x^2 - 6x = (x)(x-1)(x+6)$, and $x = \boxed{0, 1, -6}$.

Problem 5-4

Convert from log form to exponential form: $\cos x = 2^{-\frac{1}{2}} = \dfrac{1}{\sqrt{2}}$, so the least positive x is $\boxed{45 \text{ or } 45°}$.

Problem 5-5

Since $f(100) = f(10 \times 10) = f(10) + f(10) = 2f(10)$, and since $f(10) = f(2 \times 5) = f(2) + f(5)$, $f(100) = 2[f(2) + f(5)] = 2[x+y] = \boxed{2x + 2y}$.

Problem 5-6

If $z = a + bi$ and $\bar{z} = a - bi$, then $z\bar{z} = a^2 + b^2 = 5$ and $z^2 + \bar{z}^2 = 2a^2 - 2b^2 = 6$. Thus, $a^2 = 4$, $b^2 = 1$, and the 4 values of z are $\boxed{2 + i, \ 2 - i, \ -2 + i, \ -2 - i}$.

Contests written and compiled by Steven R. Conrad & Daniel Flegler   Mathematics Leagues Inc., © 1978

Problem 6-1

Let x = the number of days in a week = number of weeks in a month. Then, x^2 is the number is days in a month, and $2x^2$ is the number of months in a year. For the number of days in a year, multiply the number of days in a month by the number of months in a year. Thus, $(x^2)(2x^2) = 1250$, $x^2 = 25$, and the answer is $2x^2 = \boxed{50}$.

Problem 6-2

Clearly, $\triangle JPA$, $\triangle APB$, and $\triangle BPN$ are all equilateral, so so $JN = 2AB = 2 \times 64 = \boxed{128}$.

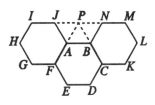

Problem 6-3

Add the exponents on the left side and equate the sum to the exponent on the right side, so $\sin^2 x + \cos^2 x + \tan^2 x = 2$ or $1 + \tan^2 x = 2$, $\tan^2 x = 1$, and the least possible degree-measure of x is $\boxed{45 \text{ or } 45°}$.

Problem 6-4

Converting from log form to exponential form, $b^2 = \log_3 x^2$. Since $b = \log_3 x$, $(\log_3 x)^2 = \log_3 x^2$; and thus $(\log_3 x)^2 = 2\log_3 x$. By rearranging and factoring, $(\log_3 x)(-2 + \log_3 x) = 0$. If $x = 1$, $b = 0$—but 0 cannot be the base of a logarithm. Thus, $\log_3 x = 2$ and $x = \boxed{9}$.

Problem 6-5

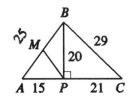

By Hero's Formula, the area of $\triangle ABC$ is $\sqrt{45 \times 9 \times 16 \times 20} = 3 \times 4 \times \sqrt{45 \times 20} = 12\sqrt{900} = 12 \times 30 = 360$. If h is the length of the altitude to $\overline{AC}$, then $360 = \frac{1}{2}h(36)$, making $h = 20 = BP$. Therefore, $\overline{BP} \perp \overline{AC}$, so $\triangle ABP$ is a right triangle. In a right triangle, the median to the hypotenuse is half the length of the hypotenuse. Hence, $PM = \frac{1}{2} \times 25 = \boxed{\frac{25}{2} \text{ or } 12\frac{1}{2} \text{ or } 12.5}$.

Problem 6-6

The numbers 2, 20 through 29, and 200 through 299 together account for a total of $1 + 20 + 300 = 321$ digits. Now let's account for the remaining $1978 - 321 = 1657$ digits. Since $1657 \div 4 = 414\frac{1}{4}$, the 1978th digit is the thousands' digit of the 415th four-digit number with a first digit of 2. Since the 415th number in the sequence 2000, 2001, . . . is 2414, the answer is $\boxed{2}$.

Contests written and compiled by Steven R. Conrad & Daniel Flegler   Mathematics Leagues Inc., © 1978

Problem 1-1

The smallest number that could be used as an addend is 1. If 1 were used as an addend 10 times, the sum would be less than 20. Therefore, 1 can be used as an addend at most 9 times. Since $9(1)+11 = 20$, the largest possible addend is $\boxed{11}$.

Problem 1-2

Consecutive Mondays are 7 days apart. Consecutive even-dated Mondays are 14 days apart. The first and last of three consecutive even-dated Mondays are 28 days apart. Since no month has more than 31 days, the three Mondays with even calendar dates must occur on the 2nd, 16th, and 30th of the month. When the 16th falls on a Monday, the 13th falls on a $\boxed{\text{Friday}}$.

Problem 1-3

Both the left and right sides can be factored further, the left into $(2x-3)(3x-2)(4x+3)$ and the right into $(2x-3)(4x+3)(3x-2)$. Since the right side always equals the left, the answer is $\boxed{\text{100 or all of them}}$.

Problem 1-4

Since $\overline{AB} \perp \overline{BC}$, $\overline{CD} \perp \overline{BC}$, and $\overline{AB} \cong \overline{BC}$, $ABCD$ is a rectangle. The area of $ABCD$ is $a+b+c+d$. Since $b = c$, $a+b+c+d = (a+b)+(b+d)$. But, both $(a+b)$ and $(b+d)$ are quarter-circles. Therefore, the area of $ABCD$ is $\frac{\pi}{4} + \frac{\pi}{4} = \boxed{\frac{\pi}{2}}$.

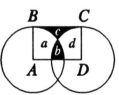

Problem 1-5

A circle cannot pass through three collinear points. The equation of the line joining $(-2, -3)$ and $(2, 5)$ is $y = 2x+1$. If $(1978, y)$ were on this line, then $y = 2(1978)+1 = \boxed{3957}$.

Problem 1-6

Method I: Since $7-\sqrt{50} = (1-\sqrt{2})^3$ and $7+\sqrt{50} = (1-\sqrt{2})^3$, it readily follows that the original expression equals $(1-\sqrt{2})+(1+\sqrt{2}) = \boxed{2}$.

Method II: Let $a = \sqrt[3]{7-\sqrt{50}}$ and $b = \sqrt[3]{7+\sqrt{50}}$. Then $a^3+b^3 = 7-\sqrt{50} + 7+\sqrt{50} = 14$, and $ab = \left(\sqrt[3]{7-\sqrt{50}}\right)\left(\sqrt[3]{7+\sqrt{50}}\right) = 49-50 = -1$. Now, let's evaluate $a+b$. If $x = a+b$, then $x^3 = (a+b)^3 = a^3 + 3a^2b+3ab^2+b^3$, so $x^3 = a^3+b^3+3ab(a+b) = a^3 + b^3+3abx$, or $x^3 = 14+3(-1)x = -3x+14$. Since $x = 2$ satisfies the previous equation, 2 is a root of $x^3 + 3x-14 = 0$. The other roots satisfy $\frac{x^3+3x-14}{x-2} = x^2+ 2x+7 = 0$, so these other two roots are both imaginary. Since x is a real number, $x = 2$.

Contests written and compiled by Steven R. Conrad & Daniel Flegler   Mathematics Leagues Inc., © 1978

Problem 2-1

Since $3! \times 5! = 6 \times 120 = 720 = 8 \times 9 \times 10$, $7! \times (3! \times 5!) = 7! \times (8 \times 9 \times 10) = 10!$. Thus, $n = \boxed{10}$.

Problem 2-2

Using the similar triangles shown, the coordinates of point C are $\left(14 + \frac{1}{4}(12), \, 4 + \frac{1}{4}(6)\right) = \boxed{(17, 5\frac{1}{2})}$.

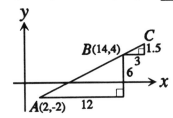

Problem 2-3

Method I: A 30-minute period with 2 mouths eating is equivalent to a 60-minute period with 1 mouth eating. The leaf was eaten in 2 stages: the 1st a 30-minute period with 1 mouth eating, and the 2nd a 30-minute period with 2 mouths eating. Therefore, the leaf could have been eaten by 1 mouth in 30 + 60 = 90 minutes. To eat half the leaf with only 1 mouth, the number of minutes required would have been $\boxed{45}$.

Method II: Treat this as a work problem. If 1 mouth needs m minutes to eat 1 leaf, $\frac{2}{m}(30) + \frac{1}{m}(30) = 1$. Solving, $m = 90$, so half that time is 45 minutes.

Problem 2-4

Taking square roots of both sides, either $x^2 - 6x + 4 = 4$, or $x^2 - 6x + 4 = -4$. Solving both equations, we find that $x = \boxed{0, \, 2, \, 4, \, 6}$.

Problem 2-5

Method I: Let O be the center of the circle. Since the length of a radius of the circle is 6, $CO = OD = 6$. Since $OP = 4$, $PD = 2$. In this circle, $AP \times PB = CP \times PD$. Thus, $5 \times x = 10 \times 2$, from which $x = \boxed{4}$.

Method II: Since $m\angle APO + m\angle BPO = 180°$, we get $\cos \angle APO = -\cos \angle BPO$. By the law of cosines, we get $\frac{5^2 + 4^2 - 6^2}{2(5)(4)} = \frac{6^2 - x^2 - 4^2}{2(x)(4)}$, or $x^2 + x - 20 = 0$, an equation whose positive solution is $x = 4$.

Method III: Draw altitude $\overline{OE}$ from O to $\overline{AP}$. Let $EP = y$, $EA = 5 - y$, and $OE = h$. Use the Pythagorean Thm. 3 times: In $\triangle OEA$, $h^2 + (5 - y)^2 = 6^2$; in $\triangle OEB$, $h^2 + (x + y)^2 = 6^2$; in $\triangle OEP$, $h^2 + y^2 = 4^2$. Subtracting the third equation from the first, $y = \frac{1}{2}$. Substituting into the second and third equations, and then subtracting the third equation from the second, we get $x^2 + x = 20$, from which $x = 4$.

Problem 2-6

Method I: Doubling both sides, $34x^2 - 20xy + 4y^2 - 12x + 4 = 0$. After regrouping, this equation becomes $(9x^2 - 12x + 4) + (25x^2 - 20xy + 4y^2) = 0$, from which $(3x - 2)^2 + (5x - 2y)^2 = 0$. The only solutions of this equation occur when both $3x - 2 = 0$ and $5x - 2y = 0$, so $(x, y) = \boxed{\left(\frac{2}{3}, \frac{5}{3}\right)}$.

Method II: Treat the equation as $2y^2 + (-10x)y + (17x^2 - 6x + 2) = 0$, a quadratic in y with $a = 2$, $b = -10x$ and $c = 17x^2 - 6x + 2$. By the quadratic formula, $y = \frac{10x \pm \sqrt{100x^2 - 4(2)(17x^2 - 6x + 2)}}{4}$. Since y is real, the discriminant must be non-negative, so $-4(3x - 2)^2 \geq 0$. But this expression can't be positive, so $x = \frac{2}{3}$, and, by substitution, $y = \frac{5}{3}$.

Contests written and compiled by Steven R. Conrad & Daniel Flegler   Mathematics Leagues Inc., © 1978

Problem 3-1

Since the length of a radius of the circle is 6, the length of the longest possible altitude of the triangle would be 6 and the triangle's largest possible area is $\boxed{12\sqrt{3}}$.

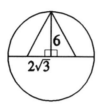

Problem 3-2

If a set has x elements, the set has 2^x subsets, so we are looking for two powers of 2 which differ by 12. Since $2^4 - 2^2 = 16 - 4 = 12$, set B will have 2 elements when set A has $\boxed{4}$.

Problem 3-3

Let b be the base of the numeration system. The angles are supplementary, so $(b^2 + 4) + (2b^2 + 4b + 1) = 180$. Solving, the positive root is $b = \boxed{7}$.

Problem 3-4

The number $.AAAAA\ldots$ must be a perfect square since its square root is a repeating decimal, and since all repeating decimals are rational numbers. Since $.AAAAA\ldots = \frac{A}{9}$ and $.BBBBB\ldots = \frac{B}{9}$, the digit A must itself be a perfect square. Since A is a non-zero digit, the possible values of A are 1, 4, or 9. Finally, since $\frac{A}{9} = \left(\frac{B}{9}\right)^2$, $\frac{B}{9} = \frac{1}{3}$, $\frac{2}{3}$, or $\frac{3}{3}$. Therefore, $(A,B) = \boxed{(1,3),\ (4,6),\ (9,9)}$.

Problem 3-5

There are only 8 winning paths: the 3 rows, the 3 columns, and the 2 major diagonals. But, there are $_9C_3 = 84$ ways in which the man can select the first 3 boxes in which to doodle. Thus the probability is $\frac{8}{84} = \boxed{\frac{2}{21}}$.

Problem 3-6

Method I: The sum of the roots is $(a+bi)+(a-bi) = 2a$. From the equation, the sum of the roots is seen to be 4. The product of the roots is $(a+bi)(a-bi) = (2+bi)(2-bi) = 4+b^2$. From the equation itself, the product of the roots is c. Thus, c will have an integral value ≤ 50 only for $b = 1, 2, 3, 4, 5,$ or 6. Hence, the number of possible integral values of c is $\boxed{6}$.

Method II: When we solve for x by the quadratic formula, we get $x = \frac{1}{2}(4 \pm \sqrt{16-4c}) = 2 \pm \sqrt{4-c}$. Since x is imaginary, $c > 4$. For b (in $a+bi$) to be a positive integer, $4-c$ must be the negative of a perfect square. We can therefore construct the table below

$4-c$	-1	-4	-9	-16	-25	-36
c	5	8	13	20	29	4

from which the number of values of c is 6.

Contests written and compiled by Steven R. Conrad & Daniel Flegler   **Mathematics Leagues Inc.,** © 1979

Problem 4-1

The subtraction illustrated at the right gives the largest result obtainable. Any other result, from a different subtraction, will be smaller than $\boxed{-2821}$.

$$\begin{array}{r} 1979 \\ -\ 4800 \\ \hline -2821 \end{array}$$

Problem 4-2

The graph of f^{-1} consists of the single point $(-4,3)$. The distance between the points $(3,-4)$ and $(-4,3)$ is

$$\sqrt{(-4-3)^2 + (3-(-4))^2} = \boxed{\sqrt{98} \text{ or } 7\sqrt{2}}.$$

Problem 4-3

Listed below are all possible factorizations of 27 and the resulting equations:

$x+2y =$	9	3	-9	-3	1	27	-1	-27
$+\ 2x+y =$	3	9	-3	-9	27	1	-27	-1
$3x+3y =$	12	12	-12	-12	28	28	-28	-28
$x+y =$	4	4	-4	-4				
$y =$	5	-1	-5	1		**NOT INTEGRAL**		
$x =$	-1	5	1	-5				

Using the information from the above chart, $(x,y) =$ $\boxed{(-1,5),(5,-1),(1,-5),(-5,1)}$.

Problem 4-4

Method I: Rewrite the inequality as $\left(\frac{1}{5}\right)^{\cos x} < 1$. Since taking reciprocals reverses the direction of this inequality, $5^{\cos x} > 1$. This inequality will be true as long as $\cos x > 0$. Therefore, $\boxed{0° \le x < 90°}$.

Method II: Take base 10 logs of both sides of the inequality $(0.2)^{\cos x} < 1$, getting $(\cos x)\left(\log_{10}(0.2)\right) < \log_{10} 1 = 0$. The product of $\cos x$ and a negative number is < 0, so $\cos x > 0$, and $0° \le x < 90°$.

Problem 4-5

Method I: A median to the hypotenuse of a right triangle is half as long as the hypotenuse. Since $CD = 4$, $EM = 2$. Since $AB = 16$, $EN = 8$. Thus, $MN = EN - EM = 8 - 2 = \boxed{6}$.

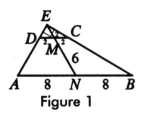

Figure 1

Method II: In Figure 2, if $DR = CS = h$, then, since $\triangle DRA$ is a 30°-60°-90° triangle, $AR = \frac{DR}{\sqrt{3}} = \frac{h}{\sqrt{3}}$, and $SB = CS\sqrt{3} = h\sqrt{3}$. Since $AB = 16$, $\frac{h}{\sqrt{3}} + 4 + h\sqrt{3} = 16$. Solving, $h = 3\sqrt{3}$. In Figure 3, $DR = 3\sqrt{3}$ and $AR = 3$, so $PN = 3$. Since $MP = DR = 3\sqrt{3}$, $\triangle MPN$ is also a 30°-60°-90° triangle, so $MN = 2(PN) = 6$.

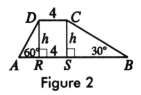

Figure 2

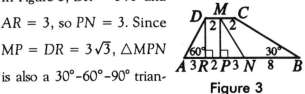

Figure 3

Problem 4-6

Let $y =$ the cost, in cents, of 1 dozen eggs. Then $(x+3)\left(\frac{y-x}{12}\right) + 3 = (x+3)\left(\frac{y+x}{12}\right)$. Clearing fractions, $(x+3)(y-x) + 36 = (x+3)(y+x)$. Simplifying, $2(x+6)(x-3) = 0$, and therefore $x = \boxed{3}$.

Contests written and compiled by Steven R. Conrad & Daniel Flegler   Mathematics Leagues Inc., © 1979

Problem 5-1

In the same circle, and in congruent circles, chords which are congruent are equidistant from the center. Since $4x + 2y = 20$ 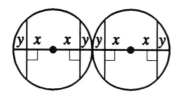 and $2x = 8$, the length of a radius, $x+y$, is 6, so area = $\boxed{36\pi}$.

Problem 5-2

Method I: If n girls live on campus, $99 - n$ girls live off campus. The 1 boy lives on campus, so $\frac{n}{n+1} = \frac{98}{100} = \frac{49}{50}$, $n = 49$ and $99 - n = \boxed{50}$.

Method II: Since 98% of those living on campus are girls, 2% of those living on campus are boys. If x is the number of students living on campus, it follows that $0.02x = 1$, so $x = 50$. There are 100 students in all, so the number living off campus is $100 - 50 = 50$.

Problem 5-3

Method I: $(20^2 - 19^2) + \ldots + (2^2 - 1^2) = (20 + 19) \times (20 - 19) + \ldots + (2+1)(2-1) = 20 + 19 + 18 + 17 + \ldots + 3 + 2 + 1 = \left(\frac{20}{2}\right)(20 + 1) = \boxed{210}$.

Method II: Using the properties of $\sum$, $\sum_{k=1}^{10} (2k)^2 - \sum_{k=1}^{10} (2k-1)^2 = \sum_{k=1}^{10} (4k-1) = 210$.

Problem 5-4

The graphs are circles with centers $(0,0)$ and $(5,12)$ respectively. The distance between these centers is 13. Since the length of a radius of each circle is 1, the least distance between the circles is $13 - 2 = \boxed{11}$.

Problem 5-5

The sum of the lengths of any two sides of a triangle must be greater than the length of the third side. In particular, $\log_2 3 + \log_2 x > \log_2 7$, or $\log_2 3x > \log_2 7$. The least integral value of x which satisfies this inequality (as well as the other two inequalities which also arise) is $x = \boxed{3}$.

Problem 5-6

Any positive number which divides 90^9 must be of the form $2^a 3^b 5^c$, $0 \le a \le 9$, $0 \le c \le 9$, $0 \le b \le 18$. For such a divisor to be a perfect square, a, b, and c must all be even. The number of possible even values for a is 5, the number of such values for b is 10, and the number of such values for c is 5, so the actual number of square divisors is $5 \times 10 \times 5 = \boxed{250}$.

Contests written and compiled by Steven R. Conrad & Daniel Flegler   Mathematics Leagues Inc., © 1979

Problem 6-1

Method I: Let's try 1, the least possible answer. We'll use x as the first of the four consecutive integers. Then $(x)(x+1)(x+2)(x+3)+1 = [(x)(x+3)][(x+1)(x+2)]+1 = [x^2+3x][x^2+3x+2]+1$. If $y = x^2+3x$, the line above is $[y][y+2]+1 = y^2+2y+1 = (y+1)^2 = (x^2+3x+1)^2$, a perfect square. Therefore, the answer is $\boxed{1}$.

Method II: Let a be the average of the consecutive integers and let y be added to the product. Then, from the given, $(a-\frac{3}{2})(a-\frac{1}{2})(a+\frac{1}{2})(a+\frac{3}{2})+y = n^2$, $(a^2-\frac{1}{4})(a^2-\frac{9}{4})+y = n^2$, $a^4-\frac{5a^2}{2}+\frac{9}{16}+y = n^2$, $(a^2-\frac{5}{4})^2+(y-1) = n^2$. This equation is true for *all* values of a only if $y = 1$.

Problem 6-2

Method I: Since $\sqrt[3]{2} < \sqrt{3}$, their reciprocals are unequal in reverse order, and so the larger one is $\boxed{\sqrt[3]{\frac{1}{2}}}$.

Method II: If two positive numbers are raised to the same exponent and the resulting powers are unequal, the original numbers were unequal in the same order. Taking the sixth power of each, $(\sqrt[3]{\frac{1}{2}})^6 = \frac{1}{4}$, while $(\sqrt{\frac{1}{3}})^6 = (\frac{1}{3})^2 = \frac{1}{27}$, and the answer is $\sqrt[3]{\frac{1}{2}}$.

Method III: $\sqrt[3]{\frac{1}{2}} = \sqrt[3]{\frac{8}{16}} = \frac{2}{\sqrt[3]{16}} = \frac{2}{2+}$ and $\sqrt{\frac{1}{3}} = \sqrt{\frac{4}{12}} = \frac{2}{\sqrt{12}} = \frac{2}{3+} < \frac{2}{2+}$, so the larger one is $\sqrt[3]{\frac{1}{2}}$.

Problem 6-3

Method I: In the figure, sides $\overline{AB}$ and $\overline{ED}$ of the regular nonagon have been extended until they meet at point P. It's easy to see that the answer is $\boxed{60 \text{ or } 60°}$.

Method II: By symmetry, extending $\overline{AI}$, $\overline{CD}$, and $\overline{FG}$ both ways will create $\triangle PQR$. Since $DP = RC = AR = IQ = GQ = FP$, $PQ = QR = PR$. Thus, $m\angle P = 60°$.

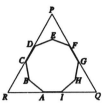

Method III: Each small arc $= 360° \div 9 = 40°$, so $m\angle P = \frac{1}{2}(m\widehat{AGE} - m\widehat{AGE}) = 60°$ (since $\angle P$ is an angle between two secants).

Problem 6-4

Use the identity $\sin^2 x + \cos^2 x = 1$ to add together all 8 trigonometric terms, pairing the terms with identical angles. This sum is 4, and the sum of the squares of the sines is $\frac{9}{4}$, so the required sum must be $4 - \frac{9}{4} = \boxed{\frac{7}{4}}$.

Problem 6-5

From the 1st equation, $y+z = 6-x$ and $x+z = 6-y$. Substituting for $y+z$ in the 2nd equation, $x(6-x) = 5$, or $(x-1)(x-5) = 0$. Thus, $x = 1$ or 5. Substituting for $x+z$ in the 3rd equation, $y(6-y) = 8$, or $(y-2)(y-4) = 0$. Thus, $y = 2$ or 4. From the 1st equation, $(x,y,z) = \boxed{(1,2,3), (1,4,1), (5,2,-1), (5,4,-3)}$.

Problem 6-6

Method I: There are 99^2 possible products, which are precisely the terms that result from the expansion of $(1+...+99) + 2(1+...+99) +...+99(1+...+99) = (1+...+99)(1+...+99) = (1+2+...+99)^2$. The sum of all these terms is $[(\frac{99}{2})(1+99)]^2$. The average term is this sum divided by 99^2, and this average term is the number of dollars the second gambler should pay to the first, which is $\boxed{2500 \text{ or } \$2500}$.

Method II: Since the expected number that each player draws is 50, the expected product is $(50)(50) = 2500$.

Contests written and compiled by Steven R. Conrad & Daniel Flegler   Mathematics Leagues Inc., © 1979

Problem 1-1

Since the length of the longer side of the rectangle is 7, $x+5-x+x = 7$, so $x = 2$. Therefore, the area of the region in the middle is $5 \times 3 = \boxed{15}$.

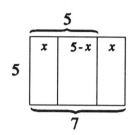

Problem 1-2

For $\dfrac{12}{x+1}$ to be integral, $x + 1$ must be an integral factor of 12. The least integral factor of 12 is -12. Therefore, $x + 1 = -12$, and $x = \boxed{-13}$.

Problem 1-3

Let $x = 987\,654\,321$. With this substitution, it's easy to see that $(x)(x) - (x+2)(x-2) = x^2 - (x^2 - 4) = \boxed{4}$.

Problem 1-4

When we factor the left side of the second equation, we get $(\sqrt{x} + \sqrt{y})(\sqrt{x} - \sqrt{y}) = 85$. If $\sqrt{x} + \sqrt{y} = 17$, then $\sqrt{x} - \sqrt{y} = 5$. Solving these last two equations simultaneously, $\sqrt{x} = 11$ and $\sqrt{y} = 6$. Squaring, it follows that $(x,y) = \boxed{(121,36)}$.

Problem 1-5

Since $x - 3$ is a factor of both, both expressions must have the value 0 when $x = 3$. Substituting $x = 3$ into the first expression, we find that $9 - 3a - 3b + 3b = 0$, from which $a = 3$. Substituting the values $x = 3$ and $a = 3$ into the second expression, $18 + 3b + 3 = 0$, and $b = -7$. Therefore $(a,b) = \boxed{(3,-7)}$.

Problem 1-6

Suppose there are x liters in the tank at the start. Then, during each of the six four-hour periods, the tank would get $4(2000) = 8000$ liters. Thus, at the end of the six periods, the tank would contain, respectively, $x+2000$, $x-3500$, $x-2800$, $x-4800$, $x-4800$, and x liters. For the smallest of these, $x-4800$, to be at least 200, x must be at least 5000. But, the tank must be able to hold $x+2000$ liters at the end of the first period. Consequently, the minimum liter capacity of the tank must be $\boxed{7000 \text{ or } 7000 \text{ liters}}$.

Contests written and compiled by Steven R. Conrad & Daniel Flegler   Mathematics Leagues Inc., © 1979

Problem 2-1

Johnny has a total of 5(88) = 440 points on the 5 tests. If he had scored 100 on 4 of the tests, his score on the 5th test would have been $\boxed{40}$.

Problem 2-2

One obvious solution occurs when $x = 2$. To prove this is the only solution, rewrite the given equation as $\left(\frac{5}{12}\right)^x + \left(\frac{12}{13}\right)^x = 1$. In this equation, if $x < 2$, then the value of each fraction is greater than when $x = 2$. If $x > 2$, the values are less than when $x = 2$; so, if $x \neq 2$, $\left(\frac{5}{12}\right)^x + \left(\frac{12}{13}\right)^x \neq 1$. Therefore, the only solution occurs when x equals $\boxed{2}$.

Problem 2-3

The equation is satisfied only when both $x+y+7 = 0$ and $2x-y+2 = 0$. Solving, $(x,y) = \boxed{(-3,-4)}$.

Problem 2-4

Method I: This result is true for all real x. Let $x = 3$. Then $a(x-2)^3 + b(x-2)^2 + c(x-2) + d$ becomes $a+b+c+d$. Now, let $x = 3$ in the original expression—the value sought turns out to be $3(3)^3 - 8(3)^2 + 7 = \boxed{16}$.

Method II: $a(x-2)^3 + b(x-2)^2 + c(x-2) + d =$ $a(x^3 - 6x^2 + 12x - 8) + b(x^2 - 4x + 4) + c(x-2) + d =$ $ax^3 + (-6a+b)x^2 + (12a-4b+c)x + (-8a+4b-2c+d) =$ $3x^3 + (-8)x^2 + (0)x + 7$. Equate coefficients of like powers of x: $a = 3$; $-6a+b = -8$, so $b = 10$; $12a-4b+c = 0$, so $c = 4$; $-8a+4b-2c+d = 7$, so $d = -1$. Finally, $a+b+c+d = 3+10+4-1 = 16$.

Problem 2-5

Players A, B, and C still have 12 games to play among themselves. Thus, they have at least 12 victo-ries to share among themselves, so one (or two or three) of them must wind up with at least 95 games won. Even if player F were to win all 28 games, (s)he could have no more than 94 victories. Player E, however, could possibly wind up in a 5-way tie. Hence, the answer is $\boxed{5}$.

Problem 2-6

Method I: If the length of a side of the hexagon is s, then the area of the hexagon is $6\left(\frac{s^2\sqrt{3}}{4}\right)$, the same as six equilateral triangles of side-length s. Decompose the hexagon into 6 (non-equilat-

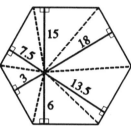

eral) triangles by connecting the vertices to the interior point, so area $= \frac{1}{2}s(3+6+7\frac{1}{2}+13\frac{1}{2}+15+18) = \frac{63s}{2}$. Since $\frac{6s^2\sqrt{3}}{4} = \frac{63s}{2}$, $s = \boxed{7\sqrt{3}}$.

Method II: Any two oppo-site sides of a regular hexa-gon are the same distance apart as are any other two opposite sides. Hence, the

distances from the interior point must be paired, as in the diagram for Method I, and the opposite sides of the hexagon are 21 units apart. Split the hexagon into six equilateral triangles. In any equilateral trian-gle, the length of a side is $\frac{2}{3}$ the height times $\sqrt{3}$. Since the height is $\frac{21}{2}$, the length of a side is $7\sqrt{3}$.

NOTE: In general, if the distances to the sides are consecutively labeled a, b, c, d, e, and f, then $a+b+c+d+e+f = 3 \times 21 \div 2 = 31\frac{1}{2}$, with a similar situ-ation in the general case.

Contests written and compiled by Steven R. Conrad & Daniel Flegler   Mathematics Leagues Inc., © 1979

Problem 3-1

Pair each non-zero integer x with its opposite, $-x$. Since the sum of the integers in each pair is 0, and the only non-paired integer is 0, the required sum is also $\boxed{0}$.

Problem 3-2

The stamps which are not on the border form an 8×8 square of 64 stamps. Therefore, the required probability is $\boxed{\dfrac{64}{100} \text{ or } 64\%}$.

Problem 3-3

If a quarter is used, there would be 4 ways ($10p$, $5p$ & $1n$, $2n$, or $1d$). If no quarters are used, there are 20 ways (which depend on the number of pennies)

$35p$, 1 way;
$30p$, 1 way ($1n$);
$25p$, 2 ways ($2n$, or $1d$);
$20p$, 2 ways ($3n$, or $1d$ & $1n$);
$15p$, 3 ways ($4n$, $2n$ & $1d$, or $2d$);
$10p$, 3 ways ($5n$, $3n$ & $1d$, or $1n$ & $2d$);
$5p$, 4 ways ($6n$, $4n$ & $1d$, $2n$ & $2d$, or $3d$);
$0p$, 4 ways ($7n$, $5n$ & $1d$, $3n$ & $2d$, or $1n$ & $3d$).

The total number of ways is $\boxed{24}$.

Problem 3-4

Let the center of the circle be O. Using central angles, $m\angle AOC - m\angle AOB = m\angle BOC$, and therefore $\dfrac{360}{21} - \dfrac{360}{28} = \dfrac{360}{n}$. Now solving, $n = \boxed{84}$.

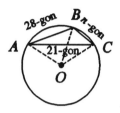

[**NOTE:** If the diagram were relabeled so n was on the longest side, then n would be 12.]

Problem 3-5

Method I: Since $\log_a b = \dfrac{\log b}{\log a}$ (to any suitable base), it follows that $(\log_x 2x)(\log_{10} x) = \dfrac{\log 2x}{\log x} \times \dfrac{\log x}{\log 10} = \dfrac{\log 2x}{\log 10} = \log_{10} 2x$. Thus, $\log_{10} 2x = 3$, $10^3 = 2x$, and $x = \boxed{500}$.

Method II: If $\log_{10} x = y$ and $\log_x 2x = z$, then $10^y = x$, $x^z = 2x$, so $(10^y)^z = 2x$. From the original equation, $yz = 3$; so substitution into the last equation of the 2nd line gives $10^3 = 2x$ or $x = 500$.

Problem 3-6

From the given equations, $x = y^2$, or $x = (x^2)^2 = x^4$. Hence, $x^4 - x = 0$, or $x(x^3 - 1) = 0$. Factoring further, $x(x-1)(x^2+x+1) = 0$. If $x = 0$ then $x^2+x+1 = 1$. If $x-1 = 0$, then $x^2+x+1 = 3$. When the last factor is 0, the least possible value is obtained, and this value is $x^2+x+1 = \boxed{0}$.

Contests written and compiled by Steven R. Conrad & Daniel Flegler   Mathematics Leagues Inc., © 1979

Problem 4-1

Since $1 + 2 + \ldots + n = \frac{1}{2}n(1 + n)$, we want $\frac{1}{2}n(n + 1) \le 200$, or $n(1 + n) \le 400$. Since $19(1 + 19) = 380$ and $20(1 + 21) = 420$, the largest such n is $n = \boxed{19}$.

Problem 4-2

Since $ax = bx$, $x(a-b) = 0$. Since $a \ne b$, $a-b \ne 0$, and x must equal 0. Thus, $3(a-b)^x = 3(a-b)^0 = \boxed{3}$.

Problem 4-3

Method I: Since $\tan x = \dfrac{1}{\cot x}$ and $\cot x = \dfrac{1}{\tan x}$, rewrite $\dfrac{1}{\tan x} + \dfrac{1}{\cot x}$ as $\cot x + \tan x = \tan x + \cot x = \boxed{\dfrac{144}{25}}$.

Method II: When we add terms, $\dfrac{1}{\tan x} + \dfrac{1}{\cot x} = \dfrac{\tan x + \cot x}{(\tan x)(\cot x)} = \dfrac{\tan x + \cot x}{1} = \dfrac{144}{25}$.

Problem 4-4

Method I: The graph is a line with y-intercept -1. Therefore, the line passes through the lattice point $(0,-1)$. If this line passed through any other lattice point, the slope of the line would be rational. Since the slope of the line is $\sqrt{2}$, which is irrational, the number of lattice points is $\boxed{1}$.

Method II: If $x = 0$, then $y = -1$ and $(0,-1)$ is on the line. If $x \ne 0$, then $\dfrac{y+1}{x} = \sqrt{2}$. If both x and y are rational (with $x \ne 0$), then $\dfrac{y+1}{x}$ would be rational. Hence, except for $(0,-1)$, no other point with two *rational* coordinates lies on this line! [This is really the same as Method I, but with certain details filled in.]

Problem 4-5

The next palindrome must begin with the digits 46, and is therefore 46 064. At a 55 mph legal speed, it would have taken exactly 2 hours to travel this 110-mile trip; and the family would have exceeded neither the speed limit nor the time limit set forth in this problem. Thus, the speed traveled, in miles per hour, was a constant $\boxed{55 \text{ or } 55 \text{ mph}}$.

Problem 4-6

The area of $\triangle ABM$ is 50, half the area of $\triangle ABC$. Since $\triangle APM$ has an area of 36, the area of $\triangle MPB$ is 14. But both $\triangle MPB$ and

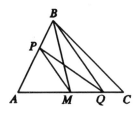

$\triangle MPQ$ can use $\overline{MP}$ as a common base. Since $\overline{MP} \parallel \overline{BQ}$, the altitudes of these triangles, from B and Q to $\overline{MP}$, have the same length. Thus, the area of $\triangle MPQ$ is the same as that of $\triangle MPB$, $\boxed{14}$.

Contests written and compiled by Steven R. Conrad & Daniel Flegler   Mathematics Leagues Inc., © 1980

Problem 5-1

The shortest such segment connects the outer circle to the inner circle, as shown. Its length is therefore $13 - 5 = \boxed{8}$.

Problem 5-2

Since each of my brothers has as many brothers as I have, I must be a male. Since my sister is female, she has 1 more brother (me) and 1 less sister (her) than I do. Thus, if I have x more brothers than sisters, she'll have $x+2$ more brothers than sisters. Since $x = 2$, it now follows that $x+2 = \boxed{4}$.

Problem 5-3

Since $i^{434} = i^2 = -1$, we know that $\left(\frac{4}{5}\right)^{-1} = \frac{5}{4} = \boxed{1.25}$.

Problem 5-4

Method I: The only numbers which are their own square roots are 0 and 1. If $5 - \frac{1}{x} = 0$, $x = \frac{1}{5}$. If $5 - \frac{1}{x} = 1$, $x = \frac{1}{4}$; so the answers are $\boxed{\frac{1}{5}, \frac{1}{4}}$.

Method II: Squaring both sides and clearing fractions, $20x^2 - 9x + 1 = 0$, or $(5x-1)(4x-1) = 0$. Solving this equation produces the answers as above.

Problem 5-5

Method I: The area of the triangle is $\frac{1}{2}hx$, with h the altitude to the side of length x. Since the area is x, $\frac{1}{2}hx = x$, so $h = 2$. For this to be true, the altitude and the side of length 2 must be the same. Thus, the triangle is a right triangle. Finally, by the Pythagorean Theorem, $x = \boxed{\sqrt{5}}$.

Method II: The area of the triangle is $\frac{1}{2}(2)(x)\sin\theta$ with θ the angle between the sides with lengths 2 and x. Therefore $\frac{1}{2}(2)(x)(\sin\theta) = x$, and $\sin\theta = 1$. The triangle is a right triangle whose hypotenuse is 3. By the Pythagorean Theorem, the value of x is $\sqrt{5}$.

Problem 5-6

Method I: Rewrite the original equations as $(x^a)(y^b) = \left(\frac{3}{4}\right)^a\left(\frac{4}{3}\right)^b$ and $(x^b)(y^a) = \left(\frac{3}{4}\right)^b\left(\frac{4}{3}\right)^a$. By observation, $(x,y) = \boxed{\left(\frac{3}{4}, \frac{4}{3}\right)}$.

Method II: Multiplying the equations, $x^a x^b y^a y^b = (xy)^{a+b} = \left(\frac{3}{4}\right)^{a-b}\left(\frac{3}{4}\right)^{b-a} = \left(\frac{3}{4}\right)^0 = 1$. But $(xy)^{a+b} = 1$ will be true for *all* real values of a and b if and only if $xy = 1$. Therefore $y = \frac{1}{x}$. The first equation becomes $(x^a)\left(\frac{1}{x}\right)^b = x^{a-b} = \left(\frac{3}{4}\right)^{a-b}$, so $x = \frac{3}{4}$, $y = \frac{4}{3}$, and $(x,y) = \left(\frac{3}{4}, \frac{4}{3}\right)$.

Method III: The equations are true for *all* values of a and b, so it makes life easier if specific values are assigned to a and b. If we let $a = 1$ and $b = 0$, we immediately get $(x,y) = \left(\frac{3}{4}, \frac{4}{3}\right)$.

Contests written and compiled by Steven R. Conrad & Daniel Flegler   Mathematics Leagues Inc., © 1980

Problem 6-1

The value of x dimes is the same as the value of $2x$ nickels. Thus, the value of the nickels is the same as the value of the dimes, $\boxed{\$5}$.

Problem 6-2

Method I: Since $ab+bc+cd+da$ factors into $(a+c)(b+d)$, the only values the expression can possibly have are, in increasing size order, $3\times7 = 21$, $4\times 6 = 24$, and $5\times5 = \boxed{25}$.

Method II: When we form every possible product of 2 of the 4 numbers, we get the 6 expressions $ab+ac+ad+bc+bd+cd$. In some order, this must equal $1\times2 + 1\times3 + 1\times4 + 2\times3 + 2\times4 + 2\times4 = 35$. Thus, the expression to be maximized is $35-(ac+bd)$. Of the possible values of $(ac+bd)$, the minimum is 10, so the maximum value of the original expression is 25.

Method III: A listing of all possibilities with $a = 4$ is

$(a)(b) + (b)(c) + (c)(d) + (d)(a) =$
$(4)(1) + (1)(3) + (3)(2) + (2)(4) = 21;$
$(4)(2) + (2)(3) + (3)(1) + (1)(4) = 21;$
$(4)(3) + (3)(2) + (2)(1) + (1)(4) = 24;$
$(4)(1) + (1)(2) + (2)(3) + (3)(4) = 24;$
$(4)(2) + (2)(1) + (1)(3) + (3)(4) = 25;$
$(4)(3) + (3)(1) + (1)(2) + (2)(4) = 25.$

If $a = 1, 2,$ or 3, the same results occur, although in different orders.

Problem 6-3

Since the longest side of the triangle is 15, $x < 15$. In addition, by the triangle inequality, the longest side is less than the sum of the other sides, so $x > 10$. Since $10 < x < 15$, it follows that the only possible integral values of x are $\boxed{11, 12, 13, 14}$.

Problem 6-4

The elephant outweighs the rabbit 5280 to 1. Therefore, the rabbit must move at a rate 5280 times that of the elephant. Thus, the rabbit's rate is 5280 feet per minute—which is 1 mile per minute. The rabbit's rate, in miles per hour, is $\boxed{60 \text{ or } 60 \text{ mph}}$.

Problem 6-5

Method I: The first 5 terms are $1, r, r^2, r^3,$ and r^4. In reverse order, the last 5 are $2, \frac{2}{r}, \frac{2}{r^2}, \frac{2}{r^3},$ and $\frac{2}{r^4}$. The product of all ten terms is then easily seen to be $2^5 = \boxed{32}$.

Method II: With common ratio r, the terms are $1, r, r^2, r^3, r^4, r^5, r^6, r^7, r^8,$ and r^9 with product $r^{45} = (r^9)^5 = 2^5 = 32$.

Method III: Since $a_1 = 1$ and $a_{10} = a_1 r^9 = 2$, $r = 2^{\frac{1}{9}}$, and the product equals $2^{0+\frac{1}{9}+\frac{2}{9}+\ldots+\frac{9}{9}} = 2^5 = 32$.

Problem 6-6

By the law of sines, the side-lengths must have the ratio 4:5:6. Using the law of cosines, $\cos A = \frac{5^2+6^2-4^2}{(2)(5)(6)} = \frac{3}{4}$, $\cos B = \frac{4^2+6^2-5^2}{(2)(4)(6)} = \frac{9}{16}$, and $\cos C = \frac{5^2+4^2-6^2}{(2)(5)(4)} = \frac{1}{8}$. Therefore, $x{:}y{:}2 = \frac{3}{4}{:}\frac{9}{16}{:}\frac{1}{8} = 12{:}9{:}2$, and then $(x,y) = \boxed{(12,9)}$.

Contests written and compiled by Steven R. Conrad & Daniel Flegler   Mathematics Leagues Inc., © 1980

Problem 1-1

Since $\left(\frac{2}{3}\right)\left(\frac{3}{4}\right)\left(\frac{4}{5}\right)\left(\frac{5}{6}\right)\left(\frac{6}{7}\right)\left(\frac{7}{8}\right)\left(\frac{8}{9}\right)\left(\frac{9}{10}\right)\left(\frac{10}{11}\right)\left(\frac{11}{12}\right) = \frac{2}{12}$, which reduces to $\frac{1}{6}$, $n = \boxed{6}$.

Problem 1-2

There are only two integers whose reciprocals are also integers: 1 and –1. Since $k-1 \neq k+1$, $\frac{k-1}{k+1}$ cannot be equal to 1, so it must equal –1. Solving, $k = \boxed{0}$.

Problem 1-3

Since $\sqrt{y} = 8$, $y = 64$. From this, $\sqrt{x} = \sqrt[3]{64} = 4$. Squaring, $x = \boxed{16}$.

Problem 1-4

Adding, we get $444x+444y = 888$; or $x+y = 2$. Subtracting the first of the original equations from the second, we get $198x-198y = 198$; or $x-y = 1$. Solving $x+y = 2$ and $x-y = 1$, $(x,y) = \boxed{\left(\frac{3}{2}, \frac{1}{2}\right)}$.

Problem 1-5

Method I: Let \$$b$ be the fixed cost and let \$$m$ be the additional cost per person (above the fixed cost). Let \$$y$ be the total cost for x people. By the conditions of the problem, $y = mx+b$; so $1300 = 4000m+b$, and $970 = 2800m+b$. Therefore, $m = \frac{11}{40}$ and $b = 200$. If $x = 1000$, $y = \left(\frac{11}{40}\right)(1000)+200 = \boxed{475 \text{ or } \$475}$.

Method II: To "*interpolate*" means to find a value *between* 2 others. This time, we'll use linear *extrapolation*: $\frac{4000-2800}{4000-1000} = \frac{\$1300-\$970}{\$1300-\$y}$, and \$$y = \$475$.

Problem 1-6

Method I: The only angle less than the average (90°) is 60°, so we're limited to multiples of 30°. The possibilities are:

A) 4 squares;
B) 1 triangle, 2 squares, and 1 hexagon;
C) 2 triangles and 2 hexagons; and
D) 2 triangles, 1 square, and 1 dodecagon.

The possible perimeters (each 8 less than the total number of sides) are, respectively, $\boxed{8, 9, 10, 14}$.

Method II: Four unit segments meet at the common vertex. Each of the four angles is of the form $\frac{n-2}{n} \times 180°$. Let the polygons have a, b, c, and d sides respectively so that $3 \leq a \leq b \leq c \leq d$. The sum of the four angles is 360°, so

$(180)\left(\frac{a-2}{a} + \frac{b-2}{b} + \frac{c-2}{c} + \frac{d-2}{d}\right) = 360$,

$\frac{a-2}{a} + \frac{b-2}{b} + \frac{c-2}{c} + \frac{d-2}{d} = 2$,

$1 - \frac{2}{a} + 1 - \frac{2}{b} + 1 - \frac{2}{c} + 1 - \frac{2}{d} = 2$, or

$\frac{2}{a} + \frac{2}{b} + \frac{2}{c} + \frac{2}{d} = 1$.

Case I: $[(a,b,c,d) = (4,4,4,4)]$

Case II: $[a = 3; b, c, d > 3]$
At least one of b, c, d is less than 5. Thus, $b = 4$. If $a = 3$ and $b = 4$, at least one of c and d must be less than 5. Thus, $c = 4$, and then $d = 6$.

Case III: $[a = b = 3; c, d > 3]$
Here, $\frac{1}{c} = \frac{1}{3} - \frac{1}{d}$. Solving, $c = \frac{3d}{d-3}$; or $c = 3+\frac{9}{d-3}$. So $d-3$ must divide 9. Since $d \geq c$, $d = 6$ or $d = 12$. Hence, $(a,b,c,d) = (3,3,6,6)$ or $(3,3,4,12)$.

Case IV: $[a = b = c = 3]$ Impossible.

Since each polygon has two sides not counted in the perimeter, the perimeter is $a-2 + b-2 + c-2 + d-2$. Therefore, the possible perimeters are 8, 9, 10, 14.

Contests written and compiled by Steven R. Conrad & Daniel Flegler   Mathematics Leagues Inc., © 1980

Problem 2-1

$$\begin{array}{r} 2 + 4 + 6 + \ldots + 38 + 40 \\ - \underline{1 + 3 + 5 + \ldots + 37 + 39} \\ = 1 + 1 + 1 + \ldots + 1 + 1 \\ = \boxed{20}. \end{array}$$

Problem 2-2

Where the regions do not have a common boundary, S has the hypotenuse and R has the two legs of a right triangle. Since the sum of the lengths of the legs is greater than the length of the hypotenuse, the answer is $\boxed{R}$.

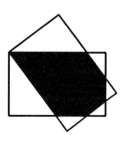

Problem 2-3

Removing the outer absolute value signs, $2 - |x| = \pm 1$. Hence, $|x| = 1$ or 3. Thus, $x = \boxed{1, -1, 3, -3}$.

Problem 2-4

If $y = 22$, x can have 20 different values (from 1 to 20 inclusive). If $y = 21$, there are 19 possible values of x, etc. Therefore, the total number of pairs is $20 + \ldots + 2 + 1 = \boxed{210}$.

Problem 2-5

Since $370 = 3^3 + 7^3 + 0^3$, we know that $371 = 3^3 + 7^3 + 1^3$. Hence, the fourth integer is $\boxed{371}$.

[NOTE: An *Armstrong Number* is an n-digit number equal to the sum of the nth powers of its own digits.]

Problem 2-6

Method I: Let $y = \frac{2x-7}{2x^2-2x-5}$. Then $x^2(2y) + x(-2y-2) + (7-5y) = 0$. Solving by the quadratic formula, we get $x = \frac{2y+2 \pm \sqrt{(-2y-2)^2 - 4(2y)(7-5y)}}{2(2y)}$. For x to be a real number, the discriminant must be non-negative. Therefore, $b^2 - 4ac = (-2y-2)^2 - 4(2y)(7-5y) = 4(11y^2 - 12y + 1) = 4(11y-1)(y-1) \geq 0$. Thus, $y \leq \frac{1}{11}$ or $y \geq 1$, and there are no attainable values of y in the interval $\frac{1}{11} < y < 1$. Thus, the least such value of k is $\boxed{\frac{1}{11}}$.

Method II: At the right is the graph of $f(x) = \frac{2x-7}{2x^2-2x-5}$. If we take the first derivative, we get $f'(x) = \frac{-4(x-6)(x-1)}{(2x^2-2x-5)^2}$. Critical values occur at $x = 1$ and $x = 6$. The points

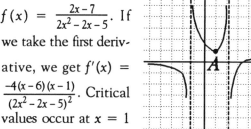

$A(1,1)$ and $B(6, \frac{1}{11})$ are minimum and maximum points respectively. [Interestingly, the relative maximum is *lower* than the relative minimum!] The graph of $y = f(x)$ has a horizontal asymptote at $y = 0$. From the graph above, there are no real values of f between $y = \frac{1}{11}$ and $y = 1$.

Problem 3-1

Both sides have integral values. The left side is an integer only if its denominator is 1 or 2. Finally, the two possible solutions are:

$$\frac{(3)\times(4)}{(2)} = (1)+(5), \quad \frac{(2)\times(4)}{(1)} = (3)+(5).$$

Problem 3-2

Draw a checkerboard. At every interior vertex, each square touches three others, so at least four crayons are needed. Color rows 1, 3, 5, and 7 with crayons A and B alternating, and color rows 2, 4, 6, and 8 with crayons C and D alternating. This shows that the least number of different crayons needed is $\boxed{4}$.

Problem 3-3

The first equation is defined for all values of x. The second equation is equivalent to the first except when $x = 3$. Therefore, the answer is $\boxed{(3,0)}$.

Problem 3-4

Draw both $\overline{AA'}$ and $\overline{BB'}$. This creates parallelogram $AA'B'B$. Label the vertex in the lower right corner with a P. Since $CP = 15$ and $CB = 9$, $BP = 6$. Then, $\overline{BB'}$ must be the hypotenuse of right triangle BPB'. Since $AA' = BB'$, $AA' = \boxed{10}$.

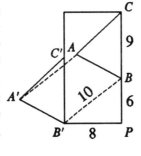

Problem 3-5

The left side can equal 1 in only 3 cases: first, the base $= 1$; second, the exponent $= 0$ and the base $\neq 0$ and third, the base $= -1$ and the exponent is even. Let's consider each case.

Case I: [base $= 1$]
$$x^2-5x+5 = 1,$$
$$x^2-5x+4 = 0,$$
$$(x-4)(x-1) = 0.$$
Thus, $x = 1$ or $x = 4$.

Case II: [exponent $= 0$, base $\neq 0$]
$$x^2-9x+20 = 0,$$
$$(x-5)(x-4) = 0.$$
Thus, $x = 4$ or $x = 5$; and both check.

Case III: [base $= -1$, exponent even]
$$x^2-5x+5 = -1,$$
$$x^2-5x+6 = 0,$$
$$(x-3)(x-2) = 0.$$
Thus, $x = 2$ or $x = 3$. (In both cases, the exponent is an even integer).

Therefore, the values of x are: $\boxed{1, 2, 3, 4, 5}$.

Problem 3-6

Method I: Let $x = n-12$. Substitute into the original fraction to get $\frac{n-12}{5n+23} = \frac{x}{5x+83}$. The common factor of x and $5x+83$ must be a factor of 83. Thus, $x = 1$ (no good) or $x = 83$, from which $n = \boxed{95}$.

Method II: A non-zero fraction is reducible if and only if its reciprocal is reducible. By division, $\frac{5n+23}{n-12} = 5 + \frac{83}{n-12}$. But $\frac{83}{n-12}$ is reducible if and only if 83 and $n-12$ have a common factor greater than 1. Since 83 is a prime, $n-12 = 83$ gives the least solution, which is $n = 95$.

Contests written and compiled by Steven R. Conrad & Daniel Flegler   Mathematics Leagues Inc., © 1980

Problem 4-1

The least perimeter occurs when 12 is the longest side. The other sides are then 6 and 8. The perimeter is $6 + 8 + 12 = \boxed{26}$.

Problem 4-2

Let p be the percent. Since $p\%$ of 100 is p, and $p\%$ of 300 is $3p$, $100+p = 300-3p$, and $p = 50$. The percent is $\boxed{50 \text{ or } 50\%}$.

Problem 4-3

The total value of all the coins is 48¢. All amounts from 1¢ to 48¢ are possible, except those requiring 4 pennies. There are 9 such exceptions (4¢, 9¢, 14¢, 19¢, ..., 39¢, 44¢). Therefore, the number of different amounts is $48-9 = \boxed{39}$.

Problem 4-4

Let $(x+y) + (x-y)i = -1+7i$. Equate the real parts: $x+y = -1$. Equate the imaginary parts: $x-y = 7$. Solving, we find that $(x,y) = \boxed{(3,-4)}$.

Problem 4-5

Of the inequalities, $0 \le x < 1$ and $0 \le y < 1$, only one, can be satisfied. If $0 \le x < 1$ is satisfied, then $1 \le y < 2$ or $-1 \le y < 0$. On the other hand, if $0 \le y < 1$, then $1 \le x < 2$ or $-1 \le x < 0$. Therefore the area of the region, shown at the right is $\boxed{4}$.

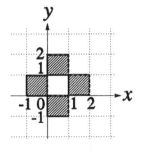

Problem 4-6

Method I: If the roots of the polynomial equation $f(x) = 0$ are a, b, c, then, by the factor theorem,

[1] $f(x) = (x-a)(x-b)(x-c)$.

The sum of the roots of $x^3+qx^2+rx+s = 0$ is $-q$, so the sum of the roots of $x^3-2x^2+3x+4 = 0$ is 2; that is, $a+b+c = 2$. Therefore, $a+b = 2-c$, $a+c = 2-b$, $b+c = 2-a$, and, finally,

[2] $(a+b)(a+c)(b+c) = (2-c)(2-b)(2-a)$.

From **[1]**, $f(2) = (2-a)(2-b)(2-c)$.

From **[2]**, $f(2) = (a+b)(a+c)(b+c)$.

Since $f(x) = x^3-2x^2+3x+4$, it follows that $f(2) = 2^3-2(2)^2+3(2) +4 = \boxed{10}$.

Method II: Note that $(a+b)(a+c)(b+c) = (a+b+c) \times (ab+ac+bc)-abc$. Since $a+b+c = 2$, $ab+ac+bc = 3$, $abc = -4$, we see that $(a+b)(a+c)(b+c) = 2 \times 3 - (-4) = 10$.

Method III: Since $a+b+c = 2$, $a+b = 2-c$, $a+c = 2-b$, and $b+c = 2-a$. Substitute these expressions into $(a+b)(a+c)(b+c)$ to get $(2-c)(2-b)(2-a)$. Multiplying, we get $8-4(a+b+c)+2(ac+ab+bc)-abc = 10$.

Method IV: Since $ab+bc+ac = 3$, it follows that $ab+bc = 3-ac$, $ab+ac = 3-bc$, $bc+ac = 3-ab$. Thus, $(a+b)(a+c)(b+c) = a(ab+ac)+b(ab+bc)+c(ac+bc)+2abc = a(3-bc)+b(3-ac)+c(3-ab)+2abc = 3(a+b+c)-abc = 10$.

Contests written and compiled by Steven R. Conrad & Daniel Flegler   Mathematics Leagues Inc., © 1981

Problem 5-1

$0.333\ldots = \frac{1}{3}$ and $0.666\ldots = \frac{2}{3}$. The product of these two fractions is $\frac{1}{3} \times \frac{2}{3} = \frac{2}{9} = 0.222\ldots$, so $N = \boxed{2}$.

Problem 5-2

The positive divisors of 66 are 1, 2, 3, 6, 11, 22, 33, and 66; and their sum is 144. The positive divisors of 70 are 1, 2, 5, 7, 10, 14, 35, and 70. Their sum is also 144. The difference between the two sums is $\boxed{0}$.

Problem 5-3

There is a lattice point at (0,0). The line's slope is $\frac{3}{2}$, so there is another lattice point on the segment every 2 units to the right and 3 units up from (0,0). The lattice points are (0,0), (2,3), (4,6), ..., (100,150). The number of such points is $\boxed{51}$.

Problem 5-4

Let $y = \frac{2x+3}{3x+2}$. Then, $y^2 + y = 6$ and $y = 2$ or $y = -3$. Therefore, $\frac{2x+3}{3x+2} = 2$ or $\frac{2x+3}{3x+2} = -3$, and $x = \boxed{-\frac{1}{4}, -\frac{9}{11}}$.

Problem 5-5

If $10^n \le x < 10^{n+1}$, then the integer x has $n+1$ digits. Thus, any number has 1 more digit than the characteristic of that number's base ten logarithm. Since $\log_{10} 25^{100} = 139.794$, the number of digits in 25^{100} is $\boxed{140}$.

Problem 5-6

Method I: Let the length of a radius be r. Since $\tan A = \frac{3}{4}$, $\tan OAD = \tan \frac{A}{2} = \frac{1}{3}$. Since $OD = r$, $AD = 3r$. Since $\tan B = \frac{4}{3}$, $\tan PBE = \tan \frac{B}{2} = \frac{1}{2}$. Since $PE = r$, $BE = 2r$. Also, if $OP = 2r$, $DE = 2r$. Now $AB = 5$, so $3r + 2r + 2r = 5$, $r = \frac{5}{7}$, and $OP = 2r = \boxed{\frac{10}{7}}$.

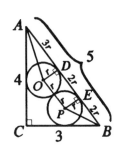

Figure I

Method II: Construct similar triangles OPQ and ABC. Then, $CK = r$, $KF = OQ = \frac{4}{5} \times 2r = \frac{8r}{5}$, $FG = \frac{4}{3}FO = \frac{4r}{3}$, and $GA = \frac{5}{3}GR = \frac{5r}{3}$. Thus, $CA = CK + KF + FG + GA = r + \frac{8r}{5} + \frac{4r}{3} + \frac{5r}{3}$, $4 = \frac{28r}{5}$, and $2r = \frac{10}{7}$.

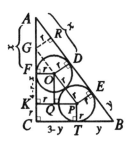

Figure II

Method III: In Figure II, let $AD = x$, $BE = y$, and $A(R)$ mean the area of region R. Then, $A(FADO) = 2A(ADO) = rx$ so $A(ABC) = A(FADO) + A(OPED) + A(EBTP) + A(PTCK) + A(QPO) + A(OQKF)$ and $6 = rx + 2r^2 + ry + r(3-y) + \frac{1}{2}(\frac{8r}{5})(\frac{6r}{5}) + r(4-r-x) = \frac{49r^2}{25} + 7r$, so $2r = \frac{10}{7}$.

Method IV: With $\overline{SH}$ the common tangent, triangles BHS, BCA, and WHA are similar triangles with congruent inscribed circles—so they're congruent triangles. Thus, $BH{:}HA = 3{:}4$. Since $BA = 5$, $BH = \frac{15}{7}$, and $HA = \frac{20}{7} = HS$. Thus, $BS = \frac{25}{7}$. In a 3-4-5 triangle, the inscribed circle's radius is 1, so triangle BHS's inradius is $\frac{5}{7}$.

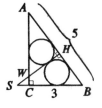

Figure III

Comment: In a chain of n such circles,
$$r = \frac{abc}{[c(a+b+c) + 2ab(n-1)]}.$$

Contests written and compiled by Steven R. Conrad & Daniel Flegler   Mathematics Leagues Inc., © 1981

Problem 6-1

Let the regular price of one widget be w¢. In cents, the price of three widgets is $2w+1$ and the price of nine widgets is $6w+3$. Since nine widgets cost 45¢, $6w+3 = 45$, $w = 7$, and the answer is $\boxed{7 \text{ or } 7¢}$.

Problem 6-2

Since $4^{20} = (2^2)^{20} = 2^{40}$, we have $\dfrac{2^{40}}{4^{20}} = \dfrac{2^{40}}{2^{40}} = \boxed{1}$.

Problem 6-3

The legs can be no smaller than 1 and 1, in which case the length of the hypotenuse is $\sqrt{2}$. Thus, $a+b+c = (1)^2+(1)^2+(\sqrt{2})^2 = \boxed{4}$.

Problem 6-4

An obvious solution is $x = 3$. If $x \neq 3$, divide both sides by $x-3$. the result is $x^2+4x+4 = 1$. The solutions of this equation are -1, -3, so $x = \boxed{3, -1, -3}$.

Problem 6-5

Multiply the 2nd equation by 3 and add the result to the 1st to get $x^3+3x^2y+3xy^2+y^2 = (x+y)^3 = 1000$, from which $x+y = 10$. Since $xy(x+y) = 200$, $xy = 20$. Substituting $x+y = 10$ into $xy = 20$, $x(10-x) = 20$. Since x is less than y, $(x,y) = \boxed{(5-\sqrt{5}, 5+\sqrt{5})}$.

Problem 6-6

Let the lengths of the sides be a, 16, and c, and let $\cos C = -\frac{1}{4}$. By the law of cosines,

$$c^2 = a^2+256+8a$$
$$= (a+4)^2+240.$$

Thus,

$$c^2-(a+4)^2 = 240, \text{ or}$$
$$(c+a+4)(c-a-4) = 240.$$

Both factors on the left are integral. Factor 240 into integers, equating the larger factor of 240 to $(c+a+4)$ and the smaller factor to $(c-a-4)$. The chart below includes all pairs of factors which make both a and c positive integers:

$c+a+4 =$	120	60	40	30	24
$c-a-4 =$	2	4	6	8	10

Solving the resulting 5 pairs of equations for (a,c), the solutions are, respectively, $(55,61)$, $(24,32)$, $(13,23)$, $(7,19)$, and $(3,17)$. The corresponding perimeters are: $\boxed{132, 72, 52, 42, 36}$.

Contests written and compiled by Steven R. Conrad & Daniel Flegler   Mathematics Leagues Inc., © 1981

Problem 1-1

Expand the left-hand side to get $x^2+ax+3x+3a = x^2+bx-15$. Simplifying, we get $(a+3)x+3a = bx-15$. Setting the coefficients of x equal, $a+3 = b$. Setting the remaining two terms equal, $3a = -15$. Solving, $(a,b) = \boxed{(-5,-2)}$.

Problem 1-2

Let the dimensions of each of the nine congruent rectangles be x and y. Since $9xy = 180$,

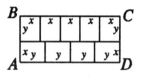

$xy = 20$. In the diagram, $AD = BC$, so $5x = 4y$, or $x = \frac{4y}{5}$. Since $xy = 20$, $\frac{4y^2}{5} = 20$ and $y = 5$. Then, since $x = \frac{4y}{5}$, $x = 4$. The perimeter of $ABCD$ (as shown) is $7x+6y = (7)(4)+(6)(5) = \boxed{58}$.

Problem 1-3

Method I: Rearranging terms, $\frac{x}{2} - \frac{x}{3} = \frac{3}{x} - \frac{2}{x}$ or $\frac{x}{6} = \frac{1}{x}$. Hence, $x^2 = 6$ and $x = \boxed{\pm\sqrt{6}}$.

Method II: Clearing fractions, we get $12+3x^2 = 18+2x^2$, $x^2 = 6$, $x = \pm\sqrt{6}$.

Problem 1-4

If a square is between 4 million and 9 million, its square root is between 2 thousand and 3 thousand. The number of such integers is $\boxed{999}$.

Problem 1-5

The largest box is not empty. It contains 10 smaller boxes. Since exactly 6 boxes are not empty, 5 of the 10 smaller boxes are empty. The other five smaller boxes each contain 10 empty boxes. The number of empty boxes is therefore $5+(5)(10)$ or $\boxed{55}$.

Problem 1-6

Method I: Divide the quadrilateral into two triangles. The quadrilaterals's centroid lies on the segment joining the centroids of the triangles. The coordinates of the centroid of a triangle are the averages of the coordinates of the vertices of the triangle. The centroid of $\triangle ABC$ is $([-8+7+13]/3, [12+15-9]/3) = (4,6)$. In a like manner, the centroid of $\triangle ACD$ is $(1,0)$. The centroid of $ABCD$ is on the line joining $(4,6)$ to $(1,0)$. An equation of this line is $y = 2x - 2$. Similarly, the centroid of $\triangle ABD$ is $(-1,8)$ and the centroid of $\triangle BCD$ is $(6,1)$. An equation of the line joining these points is $y = -x+7$. The centroid of the quadrilateral also lies on this line. The centroid is the intersection of these lines, $\boxed{(3,4)}$.

Method II: The centroid of a quadrilateral is the intersection of the diagonals of a parallelogram whose sides go through adjacent trisection points of the quadrilateral's consecutive sides.

Method III: The area of $\triangle ABD$ is 121.5, while that of $\triangle BCD$ is 162. The ratio of these areas is 3:4. The centroid of $\triangle ABD$ is $(-1,8)$, while that of $\triangle BCD$ is $(6,1)$. Assign a mass value of 121.5 to the centroid of $\triangle ABD$ and a mass of 162 to $\triangle BCD$. The centroid of the quadrilateral lies $(121.5)/(121.5+162) = 3/7$ of the way from $(6,1)$ to $(-1,8)$—at $(3,4)$.

Contests written and compiled by Steven R. Conrad & Daniel Flegler   Mathematics Leagues Inc., © 1981

Problem 2-1

If we let x be the number of each type of coin, then $0.05x + 0.10x + 0.25x = 10$, $0.40x = 10$, and $x = \boxed{25}$.

Problem 2-2

The area of right triangle AED is $\frac{1}{2}(3)(4) = 6$. An altitude dropped from E shows that the area of rectangle $ABCD$ is twice that of triangle AED, so the area of rectangle $ABCD$ is $\boxed{12}$.

Problem 2-3

An odd number of odd integers has a sum which is odd. An even number of odd integers has a sum which is even. If all 1981 integers were odd, their sum would be odd. Since their sum is even, at least one must be even. Hence, the maximum possible number of odd integers used is $\boxed{1980}$.

[**NOTE:** One such set contains the integer 1982 and all the odd integers from −1979 through 1979.]

Problem 2-4

The inequality is equivalent to $8 < 3x+4 < 32$, or $-32 < 3x+4 < -8$. Solve each inequality to get $\frac{4}{3} < x < \frac{28}{3}$, or $-12 < x < -4$. Integers satisfying the first inequality are 2, 3, 4, 5, 6, 7, 8, 9. Integers satisfying the second inequality are −11, −10, −9, −8, −7, −6, and −5. The number of integers satisfying the given inequality is $\boxed{15}$.

Problem 2-5

Method I: Factor the 1st equation to get $(4^x - 4^y)(4^x + 4^y) = 192$. Since $4^x - 4^y = 8$, $4^x + 4^y = 24$. Add to get $4^x = 16$, $4^y = 8$, $(x,y) = \boxed{\left(2, \frac{3}{2}\right)}$.

Method II: The second equation says that 8 is the difference of two powers of 2. Since $16 - 8 = 8$, $4^x = 16$ and $4^y = 8$ suggest that $(x,y) = \left(2, \frac{3}{2}\right)$, and this checks in the first equation.

Problem 2-6

Method I: Join the sphere's center to each of the 4 vertices of the tetrahedron. This creates 4 congruent pyramids. The volume of each pyramid is $\frac{1}{4}$ the volume of the regular tetrahedron. Each pyramid has a face in common with the tetrahedron, so each has an altitude to that face whose length is $\frac{1}{4}$ that of an altitude of the tetrahedron. This altitude in each pyramid is a radius of the inscribed sphere, and its length is $\boxed{9}$.

Method II: The sphere is tangent to each face at the intersection of that face's medians. Take a cross-section through the center of the sphere and one median of the base triangle to get the diagram at the right. By similar triangles, $\frac{r}{36-r} = \frac{x}{3x} = \frac{1}{3}$, so $r = 9$.

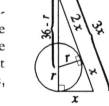

Method III: Use *Mass Points*. The center of mass of the sphere is the center of mass of the tetrahedron. Assign a mass of 1 to each vertex of the tetrahedron. Then, a mass of 3 is concentrated at the centroid of the base triangle, and a mass of 1 is at the opposite vertex. Thus, the center of the sphere is at the point nearest the face that divides the altitude in the ratio 3:1.

Contests written and compiled by Steven R. Conrad & Daniel Flegler   Mathematics Leagues Inc., © 1981

Problem 3-1

To maximize this product, let one number's first digit be the largest digit given, and let the other number's first digit be the next largest digit given. Choose the second digit such that the resulting numbers have as small a difference as possible. Since 91 and 82 are closer than 92 and 81, the maximum product is $91 \times 82 = \boxed{7462}$.

Problem 3-2

Method I: The respective diagonal lengths of squares I, II, and III are 2, 2, and $2\sqrt{2}$. The area of square IV is $(2\sqrt{2})^2 = \boxed{8}$.

Method II: In the accompanying diagram, the smaller square contains 2 triangles, while the larger square, whose side is a diagonal of the smaller, contains 4 triangles. Each square is thus twice the area of the one before it, so the area of square IV $= 2 \times 2 \times 2 \times 1 = 8$.

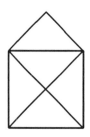

Problem 3-3

Method I: Simplifying, $14x - 3y = 4x + 8y$ from which

$$x = \frac{11y}{10}, \text{ and } \frac{x+y}{x-y} = \frac{\frac{11y}{10}+y}{\frac{11y}{10}-y} = \frac{\frac{21y}{10}}{\frac{y}{10}} = \boxed{21}.$$

Method II: Using proportion properties, $\frac{x}{11} = \frac{y}{10} = \frac{x+y}{11+10} = \frac{x-y}{11-10}$, so $\frac{x+y}{x-y} = 21$.

Problem 3-4

Since $3^{2x+3} = 3^{2x}(3^3) = 3^3(3^x)^2 = 27(3^x)^2$, and since $3^x = 5$, the value sought is $(27)(5)^2 = \boxed{675}$.

Problem 3-5

Slim will draw 25 of the 51 cards remaining. Hence, the probability that Slim will draw the ace of spades is $\boxed{\frac{25}{51}}$.

Problem 3-6

Method I: Rationalize the numerator of the left side and we'll get $\frac{x^2-x}{(x-\sqrt{x})^2} = \frac{81}{4}(x^2-x)$. Since $x \neq 0$ or 1, divide both sides by x^2-x. From $(x-\sqrt{x})^2 = \frac{4}{81}$, we get $x-\sqrt{x} = \pm\frac{2}{9}$. For rational solutions, we must solve $x-\sqrt{x} = -\frac{2}{9}$. One method: $9x - 9\sqrt{x} + 2 = 0$, or $(3\sqrt{x}-2)(3\sqrt{x}-1) = 0$. Thus, $\sqrt{x} = \boxed{\frac{1}{9}, \frac{4}{9}}$.

Method II: If $x = y^2$, then $\frac{y^2+y}{y^2-y} = \frac{81y^2(y^2-1)}{4}$, from which $\frac{1}{y-1} = \frac{81y^2(y^2-1)}{4}$, or $y^2(y-1)^2 = \frac{4}{81}$. Take square roots to get $y(y-1) = \pm\frac{2}{9}$. For rational solutions, use only the value $-\frac{2}{9}$, so $y = \frac{1}{3}, \frac{2}{3}$. Since $x = y^2$, it follows that $x = \frac{1}{9}, \frac{4}{9}$.

Contests written and compiled by Steven R. Conrad & Daniel Flegler   Mathematics Leagues Inc., © 1982

Problem 4-1

Method I: 111 111 111 is between 10^8 and 2×10^8, so its square is between 10^{16} and 4×10^{16}. The number of digits in its square is $\boxed{17}$.

Method II: Using a pattern approach, 1^2 has 1 digit. Next, 11 has 2 digits, and the middle digit of $11^2 = 121$ is a 2. Next, 111 has 3 digits and the middle digit of $111^2 = 12321$ is 3. Using this pattern, the middle digit of $111\,111\,111^2$ is a 9, and its value is 12 345 678 987 654 321, a number with 17 digits.

Problem 4-2

Evaluate from the inside out, getting $2\uparrow6 = 2^6 = 64$, and $64\downarrow3 = \sqrt[3]{64} = 4$, and $4\uparrow2 = 4^2 = \boxed{16}$.

Problem 4-3

In any right triangle with right angle C, $\sin^2 A + \sin^2 B + \sin^2 C = \frac{a^2}{c^2} + \frac{b^2}{c^2} + \sin^2 90° = \frac{a^2 + b^2}{c^2} + \sin^2 90°$. Since $a^2 + b^2 = c^2$ and $\sin 90° = 1$, the answer is $\frac{c^2}{c^2} + 1 = \boxed{2}$.

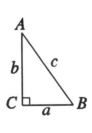

Problem 4-4

Since $\triangle APE$ is an equilateral triangle and $ABCDE$ is a regular pentagon, $AB = AP$, $ED = EP$, and $\triangle BAP$ and $\triangle DEP$ are both isosceles. In a regular pentagon, each interior angle has a measure of 108°. Since $mj\ PAE = 60°$, $mj\ BAP = 48°$. Since $mj\ PBA = mj\ BPA$, $mj\ BPA = 66°$. Similarly, $mj\ DPE = 66°$. Hence, $mjBPD = 360° - (66° + 60° + 66°) = \boxed{168 \text{ or } 168°}$.

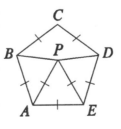

Problem 4-5

Method I: Renumber terms. Let $a_1 = 2552$ and let $a_{28} = 5279$. Hence, $a_{28} = a_1 + (28-1)d$, and $d = 101$. The 79th term of the original sequence is $a_{55} = a_1 + (55-1)(101) = \boxed{8006}$.

Method II: The 25th, 52nd, and 79th terms are all 27 terms apart, so they form their own arithmetic progression. The difference between the 25th and 52nd terms equals the difference between the 52nd and 79th terms. The 79th term equals this difference plus the 52nd term. Since $5279 - 2552 = 2727$, the 79th term $= 5279 + 2727 = 8006$.

Problem 4-6

Method I: Let M be the midpoint of $\overline{AB}$, and let P and Q trisect $\overline{AB}$, as shown. If $AB = 6k$, then $AM = 3k$. Since $AP = 2k$, $PM = k$. But $OM = AM$, so $OM = 3k$. Since $OP^2 = PM^2 + OM^2$, $10^2 = k^2 + (3k)^2$ and $k = \sqrt{10}$. Thus, the area of $\triangle AOB$ is $\frac{1}{2} \times AB \times OM = \frac{1}{2} \times 6\sqrt{10} \times 3\sqrt{10} = \boxed{90}$.

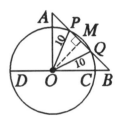

Method II: If $OB = OA = x$, then $AB = x\sqrt{2}$. Since $BC \times BD = BQ \times BP$, we get $(x-10)(x+10) = \left(\frac{x\sqrt{2}}{3}\right)\left(\frac{2x\sqrt{2}}{3}\right)$. Thus, $\frac{1}{2}x^2 = 90$.

Method III: Assign the coordinates $O(0,0)$, $B(x,0)$, $A(0,x)$, and $P\left(\frac{x}{3}, \frac{2x}{3}\right)$. Since point P is on a circle of radius 10, $x^2 + y^2 = 100$, $\left(\frac{x}{3}\right)^2 + \left(\frac{2x}{3}\right)^2 = 100$, $x^2 = 180$, and $\frac{1}{2}x^2 = 90$.

Method IV: The distance from $O(0,0)$ to $P\left(\frac{x}{3}, \frac{2x}{3}\right)$ is 10. Expanding, $\frac{1}{2}x^2 = 90$.

Method V: Since $OB = x$ and $BQ = \frac{x\sqrt{2}}{3}$, use the law of cosines in $\triangle OQB$ to get: $10^2 = x^2 + \frac{2x^2}{9} - \frac{2x^2}{3}$, and $\frac{1}{2}x^2 = 90$.

Contests written and compiled by Steven R. Conrad & Daniel Flegler

Problem 5-1

Method I: Factor both the numerator and denominator to get $\dfrac{3(1+2+3+\ldots+97+98)}{4(1+2+3+\ldots+97+98)} = \boxed{\dfrac{3}{4}}$.

Method II: If $\dfrac{a}{b} = \dfrac{c}{d}$, then $\dfrac{a+c}{b+d} = \dfrac{a}{b}$. Since $\dfrac{3}{4} = \dfrac{6}{8} = \dfrac{9}{12} = \ldots = \dfrac{294}{392}$, $\dfrac{3+6+9+12+\ldots+291+294}{4+8+12+16+\ldots+388+392} = \dfrac{3}{4}$.

Problem 5-2

Method I: Since $PQ = r$, $OP = 2r$ and $OQ = 12$, we get $r^2 + 12^2 = (2r)^2$; so $PQ = r = 48 = \boxed{4\sqrt{3}}$.

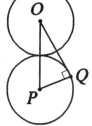

Method II: Draw $\overline{OP}$ and $\overline{PQ}$. Since $m\angle Q = 90°$, and $OP = 2PQ$, $\triangle OPQ$ is a $30°$-$60°$-$90°$ triangle, from which $PQ = \dfrac{12}{\sqrt{3}} = 4\sqrt{3}$.

Method III: Extend $\overline{OP}$ through P to T, so $OT = 3r$. Let S be the midpoint of $\overline{OP}$. Then $\dfrac{OS}{OQ} = \dfrac{OQ}{OT}$, and $3r^2 = 144$.

Problem 5-3

$3^{33} + 3^{33} + 3^{33} = 3(3^{33}) = 3^1(3^{33}) = 3^{34}$. Therefore, $x = \boxed{34}$.

Problem 5-4

Since $\tan x° = \dfrac{1}{\tan(90°-x°)}$, $\tan 15° \times \tan 75° = 1$ and $\tan 30° \times \tan 60° = 1$. Hence, their product $= (1)(1)(\tan 45°) = \boxed{1}$.

Problem 5-5

Method I: The average of the first set of 11 numbers is 15. The average of the second set of 10 numbers is $25\frac{1}{2}$, and $11 \times 15 \times 10 \times 25\frac{1}{2} = \boxed{42075}$.

Method II: By the distributive law, we see we must sum all terms in the expansion of $(10+ \ldots +20) \times (21+ \ldots +30)$. We can do this most easily by adding the numbers and then multiplying the results, from which we get $(165)(255) = 42075$.

Method III: The sum $= (10)(21+ \ldots +30) + (11)(21+ \ldots +30) + \ldots + (20)(21+ \ldots +30) = (10+ \ldots +20) \times (21+ \ldots +30) = \left(\dfrac{11}{2}\right)(10+20) \times \left(\dfrac{10}{2}\right)(21+30) = 42075$.

Problem 5-6

Method I: Let $P(x) = x^2+5x+2$, $R(x) = (x^2+5x+2)^5(x^2-7x+3)^9$, and $Q(x) = x^2-7x+3$. The zeroes of R are also zeroes of P or Q. Each zero of P is a 5-fold zero of R, and each zero of Q is a 9-fold zero of R. The sum of the zeroes of P is -5, and the sum of the zeroes of Q is 7, so the sum of the zeroes of R is $5(-5)+9(7) = 38$. Since R is a polynomial of degree 28 whose lead coefficient is 1, the coefficient of its 2nd term (its 27th degree term) is the negative of the sum of its zeroes, so the coefficient of x^{27} is $\boxed{-38}$.

Method II: Since $(x^2+5x+2)^5(x^2-7x+3)^9 = (x^2+5x+2) \times \ldots \times (x^2+5x+2) \times \ldots \times (x^2-7x+3)$, to get x^2, we *must* use 13 factors of x^2 and, for the 14th factor, we need one linear factor. There are 5 ways to use $5x$ as the linear factor, and there are 9 ways to use $-7x$ as the linear factor, and $5(5)+9(-7) = -38$.

Method III: Using the binomial theorem,

$$\left(x^2 + (5x + 2)\right)^5\left(x^2 + (-7x + 3)\right)^9 =$$
$$\left((x^2)^5 + 5(x^2)^4(5x + 2) + \ldots\right) \times$$
$$\left((x^2)^9 + 9(x^2)^8(-7x + 3) + \ldots\right) =$$
$$\left(x^{10} + 25x^9 + \ldots\right)\left(x^{18} - 63x^{17} + \ldots\right) =$$
$$x^{28} - 38x^{27} + \ldots.$$

Contests written and compiled by Steven R. Conrad & Daniel Flegler   Mathematics Leagues Inc., © 1982

Problem 6-1

The average of the first 50 positive integers is the same as the average of the first and last of these integers. Thus, the average is $\boxed{25\frac{1}{2}}$.

Problem 6-2

The given equation is equivalent to $12^x = 5^x$, or $\left(\frac{12}{5}\right)^x = 1$. This is satisfied by $x = \boxed{0}$.

Problem 6-3

Method I: Since $(x^{3/2})^{1/2} = x^{1/2} = 4$, $x = \boxed{16}$.

Method II: Since $(\sqrt{x}\sqrt{x}\sqrt{x})^{1/3} = \sqrt{x} = 4$, then $x = 16$.

Method III: Cubing both sides, we have $x\sqrt{x} = 64$. Squaring both sides, we have $(x^2)(x) = 64^2$ or $x^3 = 64^2$. Taking cube roots, we find that $x = 4^2 = 16$.

Problem 6-4

Method I: Extend $\overline{BC}$ its own length to F. Draw $\overline{EF}$. Then $BF = 2$, $EF = 1$, and $BE = \sqrt{2^2 + 1^2} = \boxed{\sqrt{5}}$.

Method II: Coordinatize with C as the origin. Use $C(0,0)$, $B(-1,0)$, and $E(1,1)$. Then, by the distance formula, $BE = \sqrt{5}$.

Method III: Use the law of cosines.

Method IV: Let M be the intersection of diagonals $\overline{AC}$ and $\overline{BD}$. Use the Pythagorean Theorem in right triangle BME.

Problem 6-5

Method I: The ratio of the excess luggage of the first man to the excess of the second to the combined excess is 1:2:6. If $f =$ the kg weight of luggage which is free of additional charge, and e, $2e$, and $6e$ are, respectively, the weight of the first man's, the second man's, and the combined excess luggage, then $(f+e) + (f+2e) = f+6e$, so $f = 3e$. The total weight is 135 kg, so $(f+e) + (f+2e) = 3f = 135$, and $f = \boxed{45}$.

Method II: Define f as before. Let c be the \$ cost/kg of excess luggage. If the luggage all belonged to one man, its weight would have equaled the sum of both men's luggage weights, so $f + \frac{8.10}{c} = \left(f + \frac{1.35}{c}\right) + \left(f + \frac{2.70}{c}\right)$, and $f = \frac{4.05}{c}$. The value of the right side simplifies to $3f$ and the weight of all the luggage is 135 kg, so $3f = 135$, and $f = 45$.

Method III: If $a =$ kg allowance, $x =$ kg excess, $y =$ excess rate (in ¢/kg), then for 2 men, $y(x-a) = 270$, and $y(135-x-a) = 135$, so $y(135-2a) = 405$. For 1 man, $y(135-a) \doteq 810$. Thus, $(y,a) = (9,45)$.

Problem 6-6

Method I: Let (x,y) be the coordinates of the focus, which is 5 units from the 1st point and 13 from the 2nd. Simultaneously solving $(x-5)^2 + (y-1)^2 = 25$ and $(x-13)^2 + (y+7)^2 = 169$, the focus lies on $y = x-3$. Substituting $x-3$ for y in either of the circles given above and solving, the focus is at $(8,5)$ or $(1,-2)$. The directrix is the y-axis, so the the vertex is at either one of the points $\boxed{(4,5),\left(\frac{1}{2},-2\right)}$.

Method II: This parabola, with vertex (h,k) has the form $(y-k)^2 = 4p(x-h)$. Since $p = h$, substituting the given coordinates, we get $(1-k)^2 = 4h(5-h)$ and $(-7-k)^2 = 4h(13-h)$. Subtracting, $3+k = 2h$, from which $(h,k) = (4,5), \left(\frac{1}{2},-2\right)$.

Contests written and compiled by Steven R. Conrad & Daniel Flegler   Mathematics Leagues Inc., © 1982

Answers &
Difficulty Ratings
November, 1977 – April, 1982

Answers

1977-1978		1978-1979		1979-1980	
1-1.	192	1-1.	11	1-1.	15
1-2.	16	1-2.	Friday	1-2.	–13
1-3.	64	1-3.	100 *or* all of them	1-3.	4
1-4.	17	1-4.	$\frac{\pi}{2}$	1-4.	(121,36)
1-5.	(2,–2), (1,–1)	1-5.	3957	1-5.	(3,–7)
1-6.	$\frac{360}{7}$	1-6.	2	1-6.	7000 *or* 7000 liters
2-1.	14	2-1.	10	2-1.	40
2-2.	14	2-2.	$(17,5\frac{1}{2})$	2-2.	2
2-3.	$\frac{1}{2}$	2-3.	45	2-3.	(–3,–4)
2-4.	2	2-4.	0, 2, 4, 6	2-4.	16
2-5.	0 *or* none	2-5.	4	2-5.	5
2-6.	4	2-6.	$(\frac{2}{3},\frac{5}{3})$	2-6.	$7\sqrt{3}$
3-1.	4200	3-1.	$12\sqrt{3}$	3-1.	0
3-2.	$\frac{4}{25}$	3-2.	4	3-2.	$\frac{64}{100}$ *or* 64%
3-3.	$\frac{1}{3}$	3-3.	7	3-3.	24
3-4.	(5,1), (1,5), (2,3), (3,2)	3-4.	(1,3), (4,6), (9,9)	3-4.	84
3-5.	12	3-5.	$\frac{8}{84}$ *or* $\frac{2}{21}$	3-5.	500
3-6.	$\frac{2\pi}{3} - \frac{\sqrt{3}}{2}$	3-6.	6	3-6.	0
4-1.	1849	4-1.	–2821	4-1.	19
4-2.	1	4-2.	$\sqrt{98}$ *or* $7\sqrt{2}$	4-2.	3
4-3.	28, 39	4-3.	(–1,5), (5,–1), (1,–5), (–5,1)	4-3.	$\frac{144}{25}$
4-4.	$10\sqrt{2}$ *or* $\sqrt{200}$	4-4.	$0° \le x < 90°$	4-4.	1
4-5.	48	4-5.	6	4-5.	55 *or* 55 mph
4-6.	(2,–8), (2,2)	4-6.	3	4-6.	14
5-1.	1943	5-1.	36π	5-1.	8
5-2.	42	5-2.	50	5-2.	4
5-3.	0, 1, –6	5-3.	210	5-3.	1.25
5-4.	45 *or* 45°	5-4.	11	5-4.	$\frac{1}{5}, \frac{1}{4}$
5-5.	$2x+2y$	5-5.	3	5-5.	$\sqrt{5}$
5-6.	$2+i, 2-i, -2+i, -2-i$	5-6.	250	5-6.	$(\frac{3}{4},\frac{4}{3})$
6-1.	50	6-1.	1	6-1.	$5
6-2.	128	6-2.	$\sqrt[3]{\frac{1}{2}}$	6-2.	25
6-3.	45 *or* 45°	6-3.	60 *or* 60°	6-3.	11, 12, 13, 14
6-4.	9	6-4.	$\frac{7}{4}$	6-4.	60 *or* 60 mph
6-5.	$\frac{25}{2}$ *or* $12\frac{1}{2}$ *or* 12.5	6-5.	(1,2,3), (1,4,1), (5,2,–1), (5,4,–3)	6-5.	32
6-6.	2	6-6.	2500 *or* $2500	6-6.	(12,9)

Answers

1980-1981		**1981-1982**	
1-1.	6	1-1.	$(-5,-2)$
1-2.	0	1-2.	58
1-3.	16	1-3.	$\pm\sqrt{6}$
1-4.	$(\frac{3}{2},\frac{1}{2})$	1-4.	999
1-5.	475 or \$475	1-5.	55
1-6.	8, 9, 10, 14	1-6.	$(3,4)$
2-1.	20	2-1.	25
2-2.	R	2-2.	12
2-3.	1, −1, 3, −3	2-3.	1980
2-4.	210	2-4.	15
2-5.	371	2-5.	$(2,\frac{3}{2})$
2-6.	$\frac{1}{11}$	2-6.	9
3-1.	$\frac{3\times 4}{2}=1+5, \frac{2\times 4}{1}=3+5$	3-1.	7462
3-2.	4	3-2.	8
3-3.	$(3,0)$	3-3.	21
3-4.	10	3-4.	675
3-5.	1, 2, 3, 4, 5	3-5.	$\frac{25}{51}$
3-6.	95	3-6.	$\frac{1}{9}, \frac{4}{9}$
4-1.	26	4-1.	17
4-2.	50 or 50%	4-2.	16
4-3.	39	4-3.	2
4-4.	$(3,-4)$	4-4.	168 or 168°
4-5.	4	4-5.	8006
4-6.	10	4-6.	90
5-1.	2	5-1.	$\frac{3}{4}$
5-2.	0	5-2.	$4\sqrt{3}$
5-3.	51	5-3.	34
5-4.	$-\frac{1}{4}, -\frac{9}{11}$	5-4.	1
5-5.	140	5-5.	42 075
5-6.	$\frac{10}{7}$	5-6.	−38
6-1.	7 or 7¢	6-1.	$\frac{51}{2}$ or $25\frac{1}{2}$
6-2.	1	6-2.	0
6-3.	4	6-3.	16
6-4.	3, −1, −3	6-4.	$\sqrt{5}$
6-5.	$(5-\sqrt{5}, 5+\sqrt{5})$	6-5.	45
6-6.	132, 72, 52, 42, 36	6-6.	$(4,5), (\frac{1}{2},-2)$

Difficulty Ratings

(% correct of 5 highest-scoring students from each participating school)

1977-1978		1978-1979		1979-1980		1980-1981		1981-1982	
1-1.	94%	1-1.	93%	1-1.	92%	1-1.	96%	1-1.	86%
1-2.	51%	1-2.	95%	1-2.	77%	1-2.	80%	1-2.	82%
1-3.	60%	1-3.	87%	1-3.	75%	1-3.	85%	1-3.	78%
1-4.	15%	1-4.	43%	1-4.	74%	1-4.	45%	1-4.	48%
1-5.	14%	1-5.	36%	1-5.	28%	1-5.	38%	1-5.	66%
1-6.	1½%	1-6.	4%	1-6.	5%	1-6.	¼%	1-6.	2%
2-1.	92%	2-1.	76%	2-1.	98%	2-1.	97%	2-1.	99%
2-2.	74%	2-2.	67%	2-2.	91%	2-2.	94%	2-2.	66%
2-3.	58%	2-3.	75%	2-3.	86%	2-3.	92%	2-3.	78%
2-4.	36%	2-4.	57%	2-4.	29%	2-4.	49%	2-4.	68%
2-5.	42%	2-5.	15%	2-5.	36%	2-5.	16%	2-5.	57%
2-6.	13%	2-6.	1½%	2-6.	18%	2-6.	2%	2-6.	6%
3-1.	75%	3-1.	44%	3-1.	99%	3-1.	98%	3-1.	86%
3-2.	51%	3-2.	66%	3-2.	79%	3-2.	90%	3-2.	89%
3-3.	55%	3-3.	67%	3-3.	55%	3-3.	93%	3-3.	77%
3-4.	36%	3-4.	21%	3-4.	4%	3-4.	62%	3-4.	36%
3-5.	29%	3-5.	23%	3-5.	21%	3-5.	12%	3-5.	29%
3-6.	4%	3-6.	16%	3-6.	15%	3-6.	6%	3-6.	5%
4-1.	91%	4-1.	72%	4-1.	88%	4-1.	96%	4-1.	91%
4-2.	81%	4-2.	47%	4-2.	86%	4-2.	91%	4-2.	96%
4-3.	78%	4-3.	44%	4-3.	81%	4-3.	83%	4-3.	73%
4-4.	66%	4-4.	44%	4-4.	81%	4-4.	64%	4-4.	48%
4-5.	30%	4-5.	31%	4-5.	92%	4-5.	6%	4-5.	74%
4-6.	26%	4-6.	51%	4-6.	38%	4-6.	13%	4-6.	7%
5-1.	86%	5-1.	91%	5-1.	91%	5-1.	87%	5-1.	84%
5-2.	80%	5-2.	88%	5-2.	81%	5-2.	93%	5-2.	79%
5-3.	60%	5-3.	81%	5-3.	62%	5-3.	75%	5-3.	83%
5-4.	59%	5-4.	71%	5-4.	83%	5-4.	64%	5-4.	81%
5-5.	50%	5-5.	34%	5-5.	48%	5-5.	28%	5-5.	48%
5-6.	28%	5-6.	12%	5-6.	38%	5-6.	2%	5-6.	10%
6-1.	81%	6-1.	90%	6-1.	95%	6-1.	96%	6-1.	84%
6-2.	78%	6-2.	90%	6-2.	81%	6-2.	92%	6-2.	84%
6-3.	69%	6-3.	67%	6-3.	69%	6-3.	69%	6-3.	87%
6-4.	26%	6-4.	50%	6-4.	56%	6-4.	62%	6-4.	71%
6-5.	22%	6-5.	38%	6-5.	21%	6-5.	9%	6-5.	55%
6-6.	16%	6-6.	32%	6-6.	4%	6-6.	1%	6-6.	1½%

Math League Contest Books
4th Grade Through High School Levels

Written by Steven R. Conrad and Daniel Flegler, recipients of President Reagan's 1985 Presidential Award for Excellence in Mathematics Teaching, each book provides schools and students with a diversified collection of problems from regional interscholastic competitions.

- Contests are designed for a 30-minute period
- Problems range in difficulty from straightforward to challenging
- Contests from 4th grade through high school
- Easy-to-use format

1-10 copies of any one book: $12.95 each ($16.95 Canadian)
11 or more copies of any one book: $9.95 each ($12.95 Canadian)

Use the form below (or a copy) to order your books

Name _____

Address _____

City _____ State _____ Zip _____
(or Province) *(or Postal Code)*

Available Titles	# of Copies	Cost
Contest Book—Grades 5 & 6 (Vol. 1) Contests from 1979-80 through 1985-86	_____	_____
Contest Book—Grades 4, 5, 6 (Vol. 2) Contests from 1986-87 through 1990-91	_____	_____
Contest Book—Grades 7 & 8 (Vol. 1) Contests from 1977-78 through 1981-82	_____	_____
Contest Book—Grades 7 & 8 (Vol. 2) Contests from 1982-83 through 1990-91	_____	_____
Contest Book—High School (Vol. 1) Contests from 1977-78 through 1981-82	_____	_____
Contest Book—High School (Vol. 2) Contests from 1982-83 through 1990-91	_____	_____

Please allow 4-6 weeks for delivery   Total: $_____

Mail your order with payment to:

Math League Press
P.O. Box 720
Tenafly, NJ 07670

Phone: (201) 568-6328 • Fax: (201) 816-0125